WORLD WAR II AIRCRAFT IN COMBAT

GLENN B. BAVOUSETT

Edited by
Stanley M. Ulanoff
Colonel, U.S.A.R.

ARCO PUBLISHING COMPANY, INC.
NEW YORK

Published by Arco Publishing Company, Inc.
219 Park Avenue South, New York, N.Y. 10003

Library of Congress Catalog Card Number 75-7167
ISBN 0-668-03823-3

Printed in the United States of America

This book is dedicated to those who designed, built, serviced and flew the great combat aircraft of World War II.

ACKNOWLEDGMENTS

This book would have been impossible without considerable encouragement and assistance from various quarters. The generosity of many individuals and organizations who furnished information is deeply appreciated.

Special appreciation is accorded to William N. Hess, author, air historian and secretary of the AMERICAN FIGHTER ACES ASSOCIATION, who continually encouraged me and furnished meaningful data; Christopher Shores of London, England, for the relentless critiques that were solicited of him; Bernard Millot of Montrueil, France, who bailed me out on occasion and plugged some holes; and Gene Stafford, author, air historian and illustrator who provided critical information when it was needed. All of these talented men made significant contributions to what is read and seen.

It was an exciting experience performing the research necessary to find the stories and develop the resulting scenes. In the process many sources were tapped for information or critique. Some may have escaped getting into my files, and to those of you whom I may have missed in the listing below, please accept my apologies.

American Fighter Aces Association; Bell Aerospace Company; Association Française pour l'Histore de l'Aviation; Service Historique de l'Armée de l'Air; Forces Aeriennes Françaises Libres; 98th Bomb Group Veterans Association (The Pyramidiers); The Albert F. Simpson Historical Research Center; American Aviation Historical Society; former members of the AVG; National Archives; 20th Air Force Association; Naval Air Museum; The Boeing Company; and the Confederate Air Force.

Denny D. Pidhayny; LCDR Tom Legget, Jr; Capt. Grover Walker, USN; Lee Pearson, Navy Department; Arthur L. Schoeni; Col.

6 ACKNOWLEDGMENTS

F.C. Caldwell, USMC; Alain Romans; Royden LeBrecht; John A. Fornwalt; Col. Ulysses S. Nero; Dr. Hal Fenner; Col. John R. Kane; Eddie Holland; Charles G. Worman; Gen. Joe Kilgore; Col. Lloyd P. Nolen, CAF; Roger Freeman; Len Morgan; Col. Kenneth H. Dahlberg; James J. Sloan; Col. Hubert "Hub" Zemke; Robert T. Smith; David Lee "Tex" Hill; Gen. C.T. "Curly" Edwinson; William E. Blurock; Lee "Kitty" Carr; Gale Hasenplaugh; Jean Coleman; Daniel T. Goggin; Leslie Waffen; Richard Keenan; Col. James Patillo; Joseph Pokraka; Col. Eino Jenstrom; Carter McGregor; Victor Agather; Gen William Skaer; Col. T. M. D'Andrea, USMC; Charles W. Cain; Bruce Bennett; Hans-Joachim Kroschinski; J. Frank Dial, and Rudolph Schmeichel.

CONTENTS

ATTACK AIRCRAFT

PATROL BOMBERS

SCOUT AND LIAISON AIRCRAFT

FOREWORD

Glenn Bavousett and Tony Weddel have done a magnificent job of joining some of the finest, most realistic military aviation paintings I have ever seen to exciting but concise explanatory text.

While *World War II Aircraft in Combat* is not a detailed history of the air action in the Second World War, it most certainly does depict, in true color, the principal aircraft that took part in the conflict. Here are the *Mustangs, Thunderbolts, Spitfires, Hurricanes,* Bf 109s, *Yaks, Zeros, Wildcats, Hellcats, Corsairs, Kingfishers, Stukas, Mosquitos, Helldivers, Vals, Mitchells, Liberators, Flying Forts,* and *Superforts* . . . and more.

They were the fighters, scouts, liaison planes, patrol bombers, attack aircraft, torpedo and dive bombers and medium and heavy bombers that fought for the mastery of the sky and the domination of the earth below. And many of those who flew them gave their lives for it.

Along with the 36 principal military and naval aircraft illustrated here are such other fighter planes as the French flown Curtiss 75A *Hawk,* the German FW-190, and the jet Me 262; bombers, including the German Heinkel He 111 and Japanese *Betty;* and the massive 6-engine cargo aircraft, the Me 323 *Gigant.*

At first glance, and even at second glance, many of the paintings appear to be highly detailed full-color photos taken in the midst of battle—where, in fact, no camera had ventured. Actually, one might say that the artist's brush captured on canvas what the camera's lens failed to put on film.

Devotion to accuracy and detail necessitated the reconstruction of each battle, using scale models. Facts were gathered from available official records and by means of personal interviews. Some of these interviews took the author many thousands of miles. Meetings with pilots or other participants in the action sometimes resulted in new information which necessitated redoing entire paintings.

World War II Aircraft in Combat is a fine book and the creative team that put it together are to be commended for a job well done!

STANLEY M. ULANOFF

INTRODUCTION

The following pages present a graphic, historical account of World War II aerial combat. Out of necessity the presentation is limited in scope. What you will see and read has taken years to research, write and illustrate. Aerial combat during World War II is so story rich that it would be virtually impossible to conclude a highly comprehensive graphic presentation.

Aircraft types and the actions in which they appear were selected to provide a loosely connected chain of events that allows the reader to trace the progression of the war, yet leaves gaps to be filled through the adventure of gaining additional information from other sources.

The U.S.A.F. is represented in thirteen of the thirty-six paintings. The U. S. Navy and Marine Corps are covered in ten, and foreign markings, on both friend and foe, are shown in thirteen more. The original canvases are in three sizes: 24 × 32 inches was used for single engine aircraft, 32 × 40 for multi-engine and one 40 × 48 which was required for the Missing Man Formation.

With the exception of a couple of scenes you will note an absence of some well-known actions, and in a few instances less prominent, yet interesting, aircraft are depicted. For example, no attempt was made to portray the Battle of Britain, Pearl Harbor action or the Doolittle Raid on Japan. These battles are generally well known and are well documented in many writings.

Attention should be paid to both the secondary aircraft depicted and when applicable the background itself. By doing so you will discover not thirty-five different aircraft types but forty-three. Also, you will find landmarks familiar to pilots and crew members.

It should be mentioned that regardless of the amount of effort expended in research to produce as accurate an accounting as possible, error may have found its way into the book. Some paintings resulted from eyewitness accounts. In some instances more than one eyewitness was interviewed and different points of view of the same action were gained. In fast-breaking combat, who stops to take a picture or even make it a point to fix everyone's position? Also, it was found that in some instances even the official record managed to conflict with itself. This in no way is intended to be a qualifying remark or to cover any error of omission or commission. As a matter of record, substantiated constructive criticism is solicited.

This book was developed by a team. About half of the scenes were completely portrayed by the finish artist, Tony Weddel. The others were developed first on vellum stock then transferred onto the canvas by the detail artist, Donovan Gatewood. Professor Neil Duncan of Texas Wesleyan College fulfilled the role of grammarian and standardized procedures regarding certain aspects of the story-lines. Editing was done by Dr. Stan Ulanoff, also a college professor and author/editor of eighteen military aviation books.

Finally, the Flying Tigers did not use the *Warhawk* variant of the P–40 as has been stated herein, their model was named the *Tomahawk. Warhawk* has been used for the simple reason that it has been best remembered under that name. Also, we refer to the Bell *Airacobra* as the P–39 when in fact the aircraft depicted was the export version which was designated P–400.

All of the primary aircraft types presented here existed in collections or museums at the time of this writing. Not all are to be found under one roof. Various museums around the country will produce all of these plus many more.

It is hoped that this book is as interesting and thought provoking to you as it has been to those of us that have been an integral part of its development.

GLENN B. BAVOUSETT

PROLOGUE

Since the late 1930s tremendous strides have been made in the advancement-of-the-state-of-the-art relating to all aspects of aviation. The "great" leap certainly occurred during the war years from 1939 through 1945. The pressure of the times served as an impetus to the aviation industry. In this period hundreds of thousands of aircraft were designed and built. Quite a few were either one-of-a-kind experimental types or were produced in very limited quantity, for one reason or another. Out of it all, however, emerged a surprisingly large number of types which were subsequently produced in great quantities.

It was a time of unparalleled ingenuity. The German Luftwaffe was not only sophisticated when stacked up against any other Air Force, it also counted heavily in numbers of aircraft and experienced airmen. Japan was no pushover either when it came to aerial might. Being a nation of islands it was only logical that they would have a vast naval armada manned by excellent seamen. Unlike Germany, Japan's navy included first class carriers as an integral part of her fleet. As a result the Imperial Japanese Navy could boast of having not only the very latest aerial weaponry but also tough, well-disciplined first line pilots and crews. Their effectiveness was keenly displayed not only at Pearl Harbor but in other battles throughout the Far East and the Pacific.

Germany stunned the world with the preemptive *blitzkrieg*. Always present was the invincible Luftwaffe blasting the pathways for Hitler's legions of tanks and fast moving troops.

No nation was prepared for either the German or Japanese onslaughts. As a result all resistance in Europe ended temporarily on

13

blood-soaked beaches at Dieppe. The road back would have to begin in England. The situation in the Pacific was equally bleak. Pockets of resistance held out unbelievably long. In the end, they, too, fell beneath the heavy boot of the Japanese soldier. Precious little of the Pacific and Asia remained free of Japanese occupation; that which did was permitted to be so not because of defensive strength but because the Japanese elected to "do business" elsewhere. The road back in Asia began in several places dictated mainly by geography; Hawaii, Australia and Burma-India, primarily.

In all of the theaters of war, however, one common objective was mandatory; to achieve victory you had to have aerial superiority—and that went for both sides. Because of that, legends of aerial combat became abundant. In fact historians are still digging into the seemingly endless stack of undocumented stories.

World War II presented a forum for innovativeness in aerial combat, both strategic and tactical. If necessity is the mother of invention, then this great conflict opened the flood gates, wide. In a short span of time pilots were transitioning from obsolete, undergunned slow moving planes to power-laden aircraft complete with excellent radar and racks of missiles slung beneath the wings. Entering the arena were also such aerial weapons as the V–1 and V–2 rockets, jet and rocket powered aircraft, suicide aircraft and piloted bombs. It seemed nothing was impossible and every day something new was tried. Pure muscle, resolution and massive supplies of material pitted against him ended it for Hitler in Europe; a pair of bombs with the greatest punch the world had ever known helped the Japanese to an early way out in the Pacific.

This was the beginning of the end for the human element playing the dominant role in aerial combat. The lessons learned by industry would soon have the speeds exceeding not only the speed of sound but doubling and tripling it. No longer would we need hundreds of thousands of aircraft—a literal handful would be all that would be necessary in future contests. From now on they would be weapon platforms guided by electronics and computers . . . the human factor in combat would recede rapidly.

What all this means is that personal aerial combat between men and machines peaked out during World War II. The days of the Aces and 30, 40, 150 or 200 "kills" are gone forever. And with them went the tales of aerial combat.

Fighters

CURTISS P–40 *WARHAWK*
(TOMAHAWK)

Fei Weing, Flying Tigers, was the name given by the Chinese to the rag-tag unconventional pilots of the fighting A. V. G. (American Volunteer Group) who stalled the Japanese advance into Burma, then saved China in a brief series of heroic battles at the Salween River near the Kunming, China, the end of the famous Burma Road.

It cannot be said that America does not have its hawks, men born with a lust for combat. Without our hawks and highly innovative leaders such as Claire Lee Chennault, our victories on land, sea, and in the air might never have been.

Men of vision, such as Chennault, knew this country was destined for war. In the case of Chennault he knew all of China, Burma, India, and Southeast Asia would fall to the Japanese unless an assemblage of highly dedicated American military pilots were not formed in Asia well in advance of our forced entry into that war. Moreover, they would require total support from home including the late model P–40s.

His bluntness and reputation of being a *prima donna* left Chennault with few friends in the military, but his overpowering, accurate assessment of the Japanese Air Force capabilities and limitation gained him the ear of President Roosevelt, who in turn set in motion the directives that would give "Old Leatherface" Chennault his A. V. G.

It was miserably slow in coming, but when it did Chennault was able to put together three of the meanest Fighter Squadrons ever assembled on the face of the earth. The Hell's Angels operated initially out of the Rangoon, Burma area, while the Adams and Eves

17

and Panda Bears were at Kuming, the other end of the narrow switchbacking Burma Road.

Chennault's first task with his one hundred or so ex-Army, Navy, and Marine pilots, who had been allowed to resign from service to sign up for a year's duty with the AVG, was to untrain them. The usual conventional fighter tactics made the P–40 inferior to the lighter more highly maneuverable enemy aircraft. To effectively defeat them meant all fighting would have to be done employing the strong points of the P–40. This meant attacking in pairs rather than singly or in groups, diving down into the highly disciplined Jap formations that would not break and run, or barrel their P–40s head-on into them but never be lured into dogfights or turn or climb. Here the P–40 was extremely vulnerable. These Chennault-devised tactics violated all rules of combat imbedded in his mixed fighting force. But, years of actual battle against these Japanese planes by Chennault himself (seventy-five downed from the cockpit of antiquated equipment) proved conclusively that his radical offensive tactics were proper and deadly effective.

Casting aside all vestiges of military bearing, the men of the AVG maintained whatever lifestyle they preferred. None wore standard uniforms, not even Chennault. Shorts, loincloths, cowboy boots, and hip-slung six shooters were not at all uncommon sights among the pilots and their ground crews. Chennault was bent on results, not tidiness or decorum.

Chennault kept his AVG mobile, constantly moving them to hurriedly constructed air strips from which to operate and confuse the orderly Japanese mind into believing far more aircraft existed than the actual one hundred.

These unconventional strategies and fighting tactics were never solved or effectively countered by the enemy. Their only answer was to pour in increasingly more aircraft which only resulted in a more staggeringly high number of enemy aircraft destroyed by the AVG pilots.

This scene captures a pair of P–40s clearing a piece of Burma sky of Mitsubishi *Claudes*, several of some 286 enemy aircraft scorched from the skies in one eight-month period of action. In the foreground is a Hell's Angels Squadron plane as evidenced by the little red lady just beneath and forward of the cockpit on the fuselage. Above is a member of the Panda Bears. It was not at all uncommon for elements of all three Squadrons to fly together.

The combined record of the AVG, 10th and 14th Air Forces is unknown; however, in excess of one thousand enemy aircraft were destroyed in the sky and another three thousand on the ground. Sunk or damaged shipping certainly ran over 2,500,000 tons while absolutely no meaningful estimate is available on the ground damage sustained in the countless strafing/bombing attacks.

Contrary to popular opinion, the sharkmouths were not spawned by the AVG. They got the idea from a magazine article showing British P–40 fighter activity in North Africa.

While the best known model of the P–40 was known as the *Warhawk,* the specie flown by the AVG was called the *Tomahawk.* Others were named *Kittyhawk.*

HAWKER *HURRICANE*

The classy *Spitfire* is remembered as the machine that fought the Battle of Britain, but in reality it was the rugged *Hurricane* that fought the hard fight.

It was *Hurricanes* that were sent to France to do battle with the much vaunted Luftwaffe. They were there all during the Phony War roaring into the skies every day, long before Dunkirk and the Battle of Britain; the *Spitfire,* the *Hurricane's* stablemate, had yet to arrive on the battle scene. These *Hurricane* pilots went up against the mighty Luftwaffe on a daily basis and as a result they gained the tactical experience they passed on to the pilots who would fight in the Battle of Britain.

Both the *Hurricanes* and *Spitfires* gave good accounts of themselves against the Germans during the evacuation at Dunkirk. By the beginning of July, 1940, the opening of the Battle of Britain, the Royal Air Force Fighter Command had 44 squadrons, 25 of which were *Hurricanes.* During fighting in France it was found that the *Hurricane* was out-performed by the sleek Messerschmitt Bf109; therefore, whenever possible in the Battle of Britain fighting a squadron of *Spitfires* went into action along with a squadron of *Hurricanes.* The "Spits" would take on the escorting Messerschmitts while the gun-laden *Hurricanes* plowed into the bomber formations. This team arrangement proved to be highly successful in minimizing losses while tearing up the enemy.

The Battle of Britain produced many stories of high adventure, courage and bravery, and brought the names of numerous R.A.F. pilots to the fore. One of these was Sergeant Pilot J.H. "Ginger" Lacey, a red-haired *Hurricane* pilot who bagged 28 enemy aircraft,

21

added four probables and damaged eleven more. "Ginger" was unique in many ways; he was on the line ready to fight when the war broke out and he was still airborne and fighting when the war ended. He fought both in Europe and the Far East. Lacey's last "kill" was a Japanese *Oscar* that he got on the 19th of February in 1945, a long time after his victories in the Battle of Britain. "Ginger" was noted for being extremely cool in combat and his willingness to get into the thick of things. His fighting spirit was well demonstrated in the nine times he was shot down or crash landed his *Hurricanes.* Lacey bailed out more than once.

One of Lacey's better days was 15 September 1940 during the Battle of Britain. On this day he rose to face the invading Luftwaffe two times and he scored four victories. One was the victory over a Heinkel 111 twin-engined bomber, depicted here.

SUPERMARINE *SPITFIRE*

On October 12, 1940, the Battle of Britain was over. Adolph Hitler had elected to postpone *Operation Sealion*, the code name given for the invasion of the British Isles, and shifted his attention to *Operation Barbarossa*, the master plan for the invasion of Russia.

Included in the master plan of *Sealion* was the movement of large forces and supplies in huge gliders designed for the short one-way trip across the channel. Both Messerschmitt and Junkers went into production of these great gliders. With the end of *Sealion* came the end of the glider program, and a lucky fate for those German soldiers and airmen who would have been in them. Without question, the legendary *Spitfires* and their fearless pilots would have torn them to ribbons.

Between the fall of 1940 in Britain and the spring of 1943 in North Africa, the great Messerschmitt glider had undergone a remarkable transformation from no engines to four engines and then to six.

In that same period of time the classic "Spit" had also undergone a few changes.

Tunisia would be the battleground for these two aircraft rather than the English Channel and British Isles. A steady flow of men and materials were being shuttled to Tunis from Luftwaffe bases in Italy and Sicily. Junkers Ju52 transports and Messerschmitt Me323 *Gigants* with Bf 109s and 110s flying escort made the low-level runs practically unmolested during the latter months of 1942.

In late March of 1943 the Battle of Mareth, Tunisia, was begun and the line was outflanked. With Rommel ill and out of North Africa the Axis defenses began to crumble under the unrelenting

pressure being applied by the British and Americans. It was during this stage of the collapse of the German presence in North Africa that *Operation Flax* was launched by the Allies. *Flax* was an intensified attempt to interrupt the Axis air transport system linking Europe and Africa.

By springtime the Allied air power in the area was such that 18 April 1943 would go down in the annals of aerial warfare as "Palm Sunday Massacre." On this day a large flight of German transports and covering fighters were caught by 9th Air Force P–40s and R.A.F. *Spitfires.* In this one brief action 59 of the transports were claimed and the top covering *Spitfires* accounted for sixteen of the enemy fighters.

Four days later, 22 April, saw the slaughter of the Messerschmitt Me323 *Gigants.* Sixteen of the enormous brutes, laden with badly needed fuel, came low across the Mediterranean—high above them flew their Bf 109 and 110 escorts. In the air for the Allies were several flights of fighters, predominately South African Air Force aircraft. Flying top cover was a Polish Fighting Team (145 R.A.F. Squadron) in Mk IX *Spitfires* plus 1 S.A.A.F. Squadron, a 244 Wing unit, with *Spitfire* Vs, while the main attack force was 7 S.A.A.F. Wing *Kittyhawks* and an R.A.F. *Kittyhawk* unit. The clash came off Cap Bon, Tunisia, and in the fierce battle all but one of the *Gigants* were destroyed by the South Africans. Practically all of the 323s fell to the guns of the *Kittyhawks,* however, "Spit" Vs from a S.A.A.F. Squadron claimed five of the big transports. The top covering Poles stayed clear of the fracas below them and held the German fighters at bay while the South Africans pulverized the 323s.

In this scene you see a Mk IX *Spitfire* piloted by the Polish ace Flight Lieutenant Eugeniusz "Horba" Horbaczewski, who was the Poles' top scorer in Africa. In all "Horba" chalked up 16½ victories in both Africa and Europe; this tally does not count his V–1 flying bombs shot down. On 18 August 1944 "Horba" shot down three FW 190s but lost his life in this combat. In the background of the painting a doomed *Gigant* is in its plunge toward the Mediterranean.

Without question the classic *Spitfire* will have its special place in our air history as being one of the few truly superb fighter aircraft types of all times.

REPUBLIC P–47
THUNDERBOLT (RAZORBACK)

Colonel Hubert "Hub" Zemke was an outstanding leader, aggressive combat pilot and an excellent tactician. He was boss of the 56th Fighter Group when it left the States and was first to receive the new P–47 Razorback *Thunderbolts.* The Group left for England in early January 1943, but it was not until April that it entered combat for the first time. Zemke brought a knowledge of the enemy the men would face in combat gleaned from service as an observer during the Battle of Britain and later as a P–40 instructor in the Soviet Union. "Hub" scored for the first time on 13 June 1943 when he downed a brace of FW–190s. He added to this score in August and September and became an Ace on 2 October. Shortly after his sixth victory he was told he would have to return to the States to be part of a Goodwill Tour. On the day he was supposed to leave England Zemke showed up ready for flying instead and led his 56th on a B–24 escort mission to Germany. On the mission he collected his seventh victory. Following is his Personal Combat Report filed after returning to base. The action took place on 5 November 1943 at approximately 1350 hours between Enschede, Holland, and Rheine, Germany, at 28,000 feet altitude. It was a clear day and unlimited with lower haze; visibility was good at altitude. This is the Report:

"As Group Commander I was leading the 63rd Fighter Squadron. Just before the combat, the 63rd Fighter Squadron was escorting the B–24's of the 5th Task Force, as given in F.O. 170 of that date. The position of the 63rd Squadron was on the right flank of the lead box of bombers, while the 61st was on the left flank.

The bomber formation was proceeding toward Munster, Germany. For some time we had been on escort with no enemy in the vicinity, when I was told there were several FW 190s coming into us from eleven o'clock (from the N.E.). These enemy aircraft were immediately picked up as being ahead by four or five miles and at our same altitude. They were estimated as about thirty staggered in depth. Since the 61st was somewhat behind on the left flank, I ordered the 61st Squadron to cross in front of the bombers and break up the enemy aircraft. We proceeded across the path of the bombers just as the enemy aircraft turned ahead to fly along the path of the bombers. The 61st caught up with us just as the 63rd was converging on the rear of the enemy formation. The enemy nosed down a bit by then, so I stepped up the R.P.M. to 2700, and the manifold to 40″ Hg. At a gradual rate, I closed up on a low FW 190 carrying a belly tank and two rocket guns. At 500 yards the enemy formation was still intact and I was afraid they sensed our presence, so I opened up with a burst of perhaps twenty-five rounds. No strikes were seen to register, so I withheld my fire for a time, still closing in on the FW 190. At 400 yards, I opened again and from that time until I closed within 100 yards, short bursts were fired. No telling effect was registered save for some occasional hits on the wings and fuselage, until at very close range I saw my tracers just going below the Focke–Wulf. The sights were raised somewhat, and the next burst blew the canopy and many pieces from the aircraft. He thereupon nosed over and went straight down as I broke to avert colliding. The other enemy aircraft had by then either broken for the deck or wheeled around to become engaged by the pilots following me. My recovery to the left and into the sun, brought me directly above the ensuing battle, where FW 190s were dog fighting with P–47s. I acted as high cover, to dive on any FW 190 who was gaining on a P–47. During this melee at least three other enemy aircraft were seen to be shot down. As soon as the engagement was ended and the enemy dispersed, the Group was ordered to return to base and I moved out."

Zemke then went on the Goodwill Tour and returned to command the 56th on 19 January 1944. He scored the first ground victory for the 56th on 11 February. His victories in the air continued to mount. By the time he left the unit in August 1944, his total stood at 15¼ victories in the air. He took command of the 479th Fighter Group where he flew P–38s and later, P–51s. He scored

another 2.5 victories with this unit and ended the war with 17.75 in the air and 8.5 on the ground.

On 30 October 1944, "Hub" was leading a mission of the 479th, something he had been ordered to stop doing since he was in for promotion to Brigadier General. But he went anyway. The flight of *Mustangs* ran into bad weather and Zemke went down. In the end it was the weather and not the Luftwaffe that proved to be Zemke's greatest enemy. "Hub" was taken prisoner and interrogated by Hans Scharff, Luftwaffe interrogater for downed Allied fighter pilots. Zemke made an entry in Scharff's "Guest Book" which rather sums up his feelings: "It was my wish to stay on the other side of the fence for a time more to run up a few more battles with a classic opponent but fate did me otherwise."

Zemke was a great teacher of aerial warfare. The 56th Fighter Group pilots racked up more than 1,000 victories, 750 of which were in the air, and the Group spawned about 40 Aces.

MESSERSCHMITT Bf 109

The "Star of Africa," Hauptmann Hans Joachim Marseille, is shown here as he scores one of his many victories over the Libyan desert. The aircraft is a Bf 109F–4. On the losing end, plunging earthward toward the hot desert sand dunes below, is a P–40 *Kittyhawk*.

Flamboyant and forever dangerous in the sky, Marseille is reputed to have run up a fantastic score of enemy aircraft destroyed—158! Of this total he is reported to have gained seventeen during three sorties in one day over North Africa. It was not that the P–40 or its pilots were that inferior; this young pilot was gifted with the ability to make lighting fast judgments as to when to fire.

Marseille died on 30 September 1942, at the age of twenty-two when he bailed out of a Bf 109G–2 after the reduction gear to the propellor fractured and caused a fire. His cockpit filled with smoke and it is believed this caused him to bail out badly and strike the tailplane of his aircraft.

The variant models of the Bf 109 which this phenomenal pilot flew during his relatively brief combat career presented no adjustment problems in his unbelievable flair for deadly accurate deflection firing. Records reveal his armorers maintained a rather accurate accounting of the rounds he expended in battle and they averaged a conservative fifteen per kill.

Enemy or not, Marseille was a fighter pilot's pilot. And Willi Messerschmitt's formidable Bf 109, when in the hands of men such as Marseille, was most certainly the deadly gun platform it had been designed to be. The 109 in all its variants enjoyed the longest and greatest production run of any aircraft; more than

33,000 of the type were built. All of Germany's top aces flew the 109 and this aircraft produced more aces than any other. The 109 is also credited with more aircraft destroyed than any other fighter type produced.

NORTH AMERICAN P–51
MUSTANG

On patrol high over Germany, near Dessau, Major Nevin Cranfill led his 368th Fighter Squadron of the 359th Fighter Group into a running air battle with a flight of Messerschmitt Me262 twin-jet fighters. During the encounter he scored his fifth aerial victory and became an Ace. The 368th first jumped a group of three of the speedy German planes that were passing above their squadron of P–51s. Just as the action commenced, Major Cranfill noticed a box formation of B–17s below him and a flight of ten more 262s beginning their dive toward the big bombers. Major Cranfill immediately gave chase to this greater threat and locked onto a 262 that had made its pass through the formation and was in pursuit of a P–51. After severely damaging a wing on the jet, Major Cranfill lined up on another 262 and commenced firing from 800 yards as he closed in for the kill. The Messerschmitt began to come apart as it banked to the left. Cranfill watched as the aircraft slipped into a diving turn, then plunged to the ground and exploded.

Mustang victories over the much faster jet became as common as those over the other German fighter planes after *Mustang* pilots gained a little air-to-air experience on the jet's performance characteristics. By the war's end practically all of the Me262's produced had fallen victim to the guns of *Mustangs.*

The *Mustang* will undoubtedly be regarded as a legend in the annals of aircraft, a status achieved by only one or two other aircraft that fought during World War II.

But it was not the *Mustang's* performance against the Messerschmitt Me 262 that earned it the honor of being known as the

best all-round fighter produced during World War II. Long before the twin-jet made its presence known among our bomber formations, *Mustang* pilots the world over had racked up a formidable tally of aircraft kills, plus highly destructive and significant attacks on ground targets and shipping. In the end, it was P–51 pilots who, after finding dwindling aerial targets, actually stalked airfields in Germany—hunting up something to hit.

Conceived by the British and designed and built by the fledgling North American Aviation Company, the U.S. Army Air Corps took the aircraft that had been ordered by Britain. The legendary P–51 rolled off the line in only 117 days after "go-ahead," three whole days ahead of schedule. With exceedingly high performance characteristics, easy to fly, and relatively forgiving, the P–51 quickly became a favorite among fighter pilots.

From entry into action during World War II until phase out from action in Korea, the *Mustang* gave a majestic and memorable account of herself.

YAKOVLEV *YAK*

The *Yak* in all its variants enjoyed a long and lusty fighting career. Introduced in May of 1940 this "workhorse" of a fighter saw service until 1953. By most estimates the *Yak* ran a close second to the Messerschmitt Bf 109 in numbers produced.

Below 16,000 feet the scrappy fighter was a terror to the German Luftwaffe. At lower altitudes the *Yak's* superior speed and maneuverability undoubtedly was a great assist to her many pilots who racked up enviable scores of downed 109s. And Russian pilots were fond of getting right on the deck and busting tanks with the *Yak's* nose mounted cannon.

Russians were not the sole users of the *Yak* fighter. The Free French, Polish, Yugoslav and North Korean air forces also employed the aircraft. It was the latter who dashed across the 38th parallel with half a dozen *Yaks* and destroyed a C–54 near Seoul, Korea. A couple of days later *Twin-Mustang* pilots tagged three of the *Yaks* ending their presence in Korea. This encounter in 1950 was not the first clash between *Yak* and American planes; it was, however, the last, and in both instances the little fighter that had punished the German so well came out a poor second against the American.

The first engagement occurred in early November 1944, over Yugoslavia. Russian ground forces had the German in retreat. The 15th Air Force was requested to provide close air support. Colonel C. T. "Curley" Edwinson's [now General (Ret)] 82nd Fighter

Group operating from Foggia, Italy, caught the mission. The husky P–38's performance was so good that the Russians asked for a repeat support mission to be flown by the same group on the following day. Again, Edwinson led his three squadrons of P–38s across the Adriatic and down into the valleys of mountainous Yugoslavia. Unknown to Edwinson a crisis was in the making. The Russians had failed to advise Foggia that during the interval between the previous day's support mission and now, Russian ground forces had advanced the battle line by 100 kilometers. Edwinson led the P–38s into the strafing attack that ripped first into the Germans then immediately into the Russians. The resulting devastation was both massive and effective. Caught in the strafing was a Russian staff car. Its occupant, a three-star General, was killed, a victim of lack of communications and a close similarity between German and Russian uniforms and vehicle color schemes. And with the P–38's speed these differences went unnoticed. A flight of *Yaks* were in the vicinity and the call went out for them to attack the P–38s still busy making strafing runs. Caught totally by surprise, Edwinson saw two of his aircraft being shot down. Instantly he signalled the squadron to disengage from the ground attack and fight their way out of the valley. During the brief air battle that ensued Edwinson's P–38 pilots knocked down four of the *Yaks* and sent the remainder scurrying away into the haze. One of the four *Yaks* that really got it was the unlucky fellow whose course took him directly over the guns of the P–38 piloted by Bill Blurock who was in a stall condition and but a few yards under the Russian. A touch of the button and the *Yak* was literally ripped to shreds. It is this moment of the action depicted in this painting.

This incident over Yugoslavia gave the United States a 4-to-2 edge in the only known aerial combat between the two powers (the 1950 engagement involved North Korean pilots). When advised that the situation was one of those unfortunate happenings that bad communications sometime foster, and after all it was the Russians who attacked the P–38s, the Russians promptly shot those involved on their end and demanded the same be done to Edwinson, the leader of the P–38s. "Curly" Edwinson was quietly and hastily re-assigned to a base out of Europe.

A bad day for these particular *Yaks* should not be interpreted as a sign of inferior equipment . . . not so. Its overall combat record

is excellent. Edwinson had superior fighters and some of the finest pilots around. It was no contest even though the Russian pilots entered the action with the advantage of surprise and at a fighting altitude of their choosing.

REPUBLIC P–47
THUNDERBOLT

Probably the last item of the design criteria for this brute of an airplane was that relating to ground support missions.

Big, barrel-shaped (the P–47 was the biggest, heaviest fighter produced by America during the war), this rugged airplane was so well built and armored that all of her leading aces survived the war. The mighty "Jug," as the P–47 came to be known, was notorious for getting you back. Not only could the "Jugs" dish it out in a real slugfest, but they could also take a terrible beating and keep on flying.

At one time or another during its World War II service life, the P–47 *Thunderbolt* was assigned to slightly less than 60 fighter groups, an impressive dispersal record. Yet, four Air Forces (4th, 6th, 11th and 13th) flew no P–47s in any of their fighter squadrons. It was the 9th Air Force that was to be the biggest user of the *Thunderbolt,* sixteen fighter groups.

While the heavy bombers of the 8th Air Force busied themselves with the high altitude precision bombing of Hitler's industrial cities, it was the medium and light bombers of the 9th Air Force which fell heir to the destruction of his bridges, barges, marshalling yards and long lines of ground combat forces. Both Air Forces used P–38s, P–47s and P–51s primarily to protect their bombers as they went about their bombing missions. And the fighter pilots did a remarkable job, as the records show.

Because the 9th operated down closer to their targets and because the fighters of both the 8th and 9th, along with their Allied partners, had done a rather thorough job in cleansing the air of the once-dreaded Luftwaffe, it followed that the day would come when the fighters would turn fighter-bombers and go down on the deck to help root out the dwindling German forces there.

Late September, the 29th of 1944, provided most of German activity for the 9th Air Force's P–47s. Hitler began moving the best that was left of his once-proud armies into the Ardennes Forest, slowly, inconspicuously moving them through the byways and waterways but always towards the Ardennes where the queen of all land battles would be fought—the Battle of the Bulge.

Screaming down out of the sky to shoot up everything that moves and some that does not, are 9th Air Force, 373rd Fighter Group P–47s. They get what they can at this river site before terrible weather shuts them off from the action at the Bulge.

Many countries had this truly fine fighter-bomber in their inventories. Among them were numerous Central and South American nations including Peru, Chile, Mexico, Nicaragua, Bolivia and Ecuador to name a few. And, of course, the big users such as the Royal Air Force, China, and Russia all had the mighty "Jug."

LOCKHEED P–38 *LIGHTNING*

Admiral Isoroku Yamamoto, Commander in Chief of the Japanese Combined Fleet, was a punctual man. It was this discipline in his character that cost him his life the morning of 18 April 1943, Palm Sunday.

Yamamoto sat in the cockpit of one of two *Betty* bombers flying a southeasterly course down the coastline of Bougainville. Above and in front of him, flying into the sunrise, was an escort of six *Zero* fighters. The group had lifted off from Rabaul at precisely 0600 hours and was now only minutes away from its destination, Ballale Island, where the Admiral and his staff would begin an inspection and morale boosting tour of the forward defenses. In strict compliance with the Admiral's schedule the flight would arrive at 0800 hours.

Four days earlier intelligence personnel at Pearl Harbor had intercepted and broken the coded Japanese message that revealed the Admiral's planned movement and the limited aerial strength. After hasty deliberations within the political and military complex, the decision was made to intercept and destroy the Admiral.

The mission was assigned to the 339th and 12th Fighter Squadrons flying P–38 *Lightnings* from Fighter Strip Number Two on Guadalcanal. Extra large auxiliary fuel tanks were moved in during the night of the 17th and installed on eighteen *Lightnings*. It was a long 650 miles from Guadalcanal to Bougainville.

As dawn broke on the 18th, the heavily laden *Lightnings* used all of Strip Two in getting airborne. In the process one P–38 blew a tire and skidded off the runway. Then, as the remaining P–38s formed up, another one suffered fuel system problems and was

44

waved off. Sixteen *Lightnings* now continued toward Bougainville to meet a destiny that would in its own way alter the course of the war.

Twelve of the sixteen craft were to provide defensive cover for the other four which had been designated as the killer group. Their sole objective was to shoot down the two Japanese bombers—regardless!

Right on Yamamoto's schedule the two groups met. Jettisoning their tanks, Tom Lanphier and Rex Barber throttled in for the kill as Besby Holmes fought frantically to release his tank which stubbornly refused to let go. Raymond Hine, seeing Holmes' vulnerability, aborted his attack on the *Bettys* to fly wing position and protect Holmes until the tank problem was solved.

From beginning to end the action consumed a bare thirty seconds. In that brief course of time both of the Japanese *Betty* bombers were downed along with three of the escorting *Zero* fighters, all from the guns of the four killer group *Lightnings*.

Shown here is a glimpse of that fight with Tom Lanphier's P–38, "Phoebe," in the foreground. Behind him is Yamamoto's *Betty* breaking up prior to crashing in heavy jungle growth. Below is the other *Betty,* which after having been virtually chopped to pieces, crashed heavily into the water just offshore the Japanese base at Buin. Miraculously, three survived the crash of the second *Betty*— Vice Admiral Ugaki, Rear Admiral Kitamura, and the pilot, Warrant Officer Hayashi.

One American, Ray Hine, failed to return.

It is significant that after this brief but devastating engagement the Japanese never again achieved a major victory, only disasters that crept relentlessly toward the home islands. Yamamoto, the great naval strategist, was no more.

BELL P–39 and P–400
AIRACOBRA

When the Japanese struck Pearl Harbor, the United States' first-line of fighter defense was composed of Navy and Marine piloted F4F *Wildcats* and the Army Air Force piloted P–40 *Warhawks* and P–39 *Airacobras.* To these rugged but obsolete aircraft fell the tough task of buying us the time needed to gear up for war.

Designed to fight a completely different generation of enemy aircraft, two of the three fighter types would emerge from the early onslaughts with good reputations; the third, the *Airacobra,* would find the going pretty tough. Designed to fight at altitudes under 15,000 feet, the sleek long-nosed P–39 was soon weighted down with so much fire-power capability that by the time a fighting altitude could be reached the battle was invariably over, and in the Pacific the *Zero* pilots simply climbed beyond the P–39's ceiling then pounced. As radical and innovative as it was, the P–39 simply could not hold its own against the Japanese *Zeros* and German *109s.*

The British were probably the most discouraged recipients of the P–39 (P–400s as the export version) while the Russians were unquestionably the happiest. Leaving the heroics of dogfighting to other aircraft types, the Soviets put the P–39 down on the deck where it belonged and where it could best hurt the German.

As MacArthur began the frustrating process of making good his promise to "return" from his Australian headquarters, crated P–400s destined for the British were rerouted to Tontouta, New Caledonia, for use by Americans who had no planes, but were now at war. As the men labored in the mud and rain to uncrate and assemble the forty-five P–400s, they discovered nobody had ever be-

47

fore met one. Obstacle after obstacle was overcome in the rush to assemble the craft, a feat accomplished without benefit of any technical manuals in only six days. The 67th Fighter Squadron could now say it was ready to fight.

In time the 67th moved nearer to the action and began operation from Guadalcanal. It was here they found by trial and error the strengths and weaknesses of their mixture of P–400s and P–39s. Reluctantly, the 67th let the derring-do of fighter scrambles go to the *Wildcats* and *Corsairs.* As we see here, they found their power to hurt the enemy was ripping into him down on the ground, appearing suddenly from nowhere, tearing to shreds anything standing in its way. The P–39s and 400s of the 67th were easily recognized by the sharkmouths they took from the departing P–40s. P–400s were left in the British camouflage scheme that was on them when they were uncrated in New Caledonia. Only the British markings were painted over.

As a part of the 374th Fighter Group the 67th transitioned into P–38 *Lightnings* in August of 1944. They were the last Fighter Group to fly *Airacobras* in the Pacific.

GRUMMAN F4F *WILDCAT*

On the 3rd day in May of 1942, three days prior to the fall of Corregidor, Admiral Yamamoto sent Vice Admiral Hara out of Rabaul and into the Solomons and Coral Sea in force. The three-fold objective was to take Tulagi on Florida Island in the Solomons and establish a seaplane base, then take Port Moresby situated in the southeastern part of New Guinea, and, finally, if possible, to draw out the remaining American naval power and destroy it once and for all.

On the first day of May, Task Force 17 under Real Admiral Fletcher had entered the Coral Sea from the southeast.

American cryptanalysts had long since broken the Japanese code and therefore clearly understood the enemy's intentions as they ventured into the Coral Sea and Solomons area.

Now would commence the strangest of all sea battles, The Battle of the Coral Sea. For the first time in maritime battle history, not a single shot would be exchanged between surface vessels. It would be a decisive naval engagement fought entirely by the opposing forces' aerial strengths.

On 3 May Tulagi fell to the Japanese, precisely as scheduled by Yamamoto. On May 4, *Yorktown* planes made several retaliatory air strikes on Tulagi that proved to be of little consequence. The 5th and 6th were quiet as both sides swept the Coral Sea in search of one another, especially for the carrier forces which were known to exist. Then, on the 7th, contact was made with the Japanese invasion force headed for Port Moresby. Immediately, *Yorktown Wildcats,* dive bombers, and torpedo planes raced to the attack; and for the first time the word flashed back "scratch one flattop."

Within ten short minutes the carrier *Shoho* slipped beneath the waves of the Coral Sea. With the sinking of *Shoho,* any further advance toward Port Moresby was aborted by the enemy.

But it was the fight on the 8th of May which would show the muscle that foretold what the outcome of the future naval battles would be. On this day the giants would clash.

It was an evenly matched battle with the slight weather advantage for the Japanese. Both sides had equal numbers of aircraft, carriers, and supporting warships of the line. The two Japanese carriers, *Zuikaku* and *Shokaku,* had participated in the attack on Pearl Harbor. Opposing this pair of leviathans were Task Force 17's heavy carriers *Yorktown* and *Lexington.* Aircraft from both forces found each other's carriers about the same time, and without hesitation attacked. *Zuikaku* escaped into heavy weather, but *Shokaku* was less fortunate; *Yorktown* dive bombers placed two five-hundred pound bombs on her deck, warping it, and a later strike added a third. Beyond the horizon both the *Lexington* and *Yorktown* were sustaining hits; the *Lexington's* damage was of such a nature that salvage was impossible, and she was subsequently sunk by Task Force 17 destroyers.

The seizure of Tulagi proved to be no major threat to our later movements around New Guinea, the Bismarck Barrier or the Solomons. A bashful Japanese Admiral had turned his invasion force away from Port Moresby, never again to threaten the place with such a glorious opportunity; one enemy carrier, small as it was, had been sunk, and the two large carriers were to remain non-operational in Japanese home waters and miss the momentous Battle of Midway.

Rising up out of the flak from the damaged but fighting *Shokaku* are two F4Fs from VF-2 off the *Yorktown.* It was this fighter type along with the world-famous sharkmouthed P-40 *Warhawks,* P-39 *Airacobras,* and British *Spitfires* that held the line fighting off the best the enemy had until the next generation of fighters could come off the production lines to enter the battle arenas.

In the decisive Battle of the Coral Sea, twenty-two F4F *Wildcats* of VF-2 operated from the *Yorktown* and twenty from VF-42 rose from the deck of the *Lexington.* The Battle of the Coral Sea proved the Japanese could be stopped. And air power did it!

GRUMMAN F6F *HELLCAT*

Occasionally, a truly superb combat aircraft fails to receive the high degree of recognition that it rightly deserves. Such is the case of the mighty Grumman F6F *Hellcat,* successor to the F4F *Wildcat* and bearing a close family resemblance to it. It was a dedicated competitor of the fine F4U *Corsair.* No question about it, the powerful F4U was "whistling death" to the Japanese. The record, however, reveals it was the deadly F6F that clobbered the aerial might of the Japanese.

Fate moves in strange ways. And so it happened that Yamamoto's northern force that struck the Aleutians during the Battle of Midway allowed a *Zero* to crash land intact. The craft was quickly shipped stateside where is was reassembled. It was subjected to severe test flights to reveal its weak and strong flight characteristics. The F6F *Hellcat* was the fighting machine designed specifically to counter the *Zero's* strong points and take advantage of its weaknesses. It was superior to the best the Japanese could put into the air. And from its initial debut in the Marcus Islands this fighting plane proved its superiority over Japanese aircraft.

Statistically, *Hellcats* are credited with the destruction of more than 5,000 enemy aircraft while the *Corsair's* score is slightly over 2,000. This is in the face of the fact that more *Corsairs* were produced than *Hellcats* and, more importantly, entered the Pacific action at least six months prior to the *Hellcat.* Both aircraft racked up fantastic records.

From the onset *Hellcats* had an insatiable appetite for enemy aircraft. Not only did they turn in noteworthy performances in the Gilberts and Carolines, but they baited, then destroyed everything flyable in and around Truk, the impregnable Japanese Pearl Harbor of the Pacific.

Came the dawn of 19 June 1944 and the stage was set for what was to become known as the "Marianas Turkey Shoot." Separated by some 400 nautical miles of Philippine Sea were Vice-Admiral Ozawa's forces and Admiral Marc Mitscher's Task Force 58, tremendous armadas of naval surface warships and airpower. When the opposing forces found one another, the Turkey Shoot began. By sunset *Hellcat* pilots had bagged nearly 400 enemy aircraft with a loss of only eighteen *Hellcats,* a lopsided victory if ever one existed and a great testimonial to the F6Fs' fighting abilities and the tenacity of its pilots.

Depicted here is the F6F–5, "MINSI II," flown by the Air Group Commander of VF–15 (Fabled Fifteen) off the carrier *Essex.* It is Commander David McCampbell enroute to racking up nine enemy aircraft over the Philippines on 24 October 1944. Part of Commander McCampbell's Congressional Medal of Honor citation for this exploit reads ". . . During a major Fleet engagement with the enemy on October 24, Commander McCampbell, assisted by but one plane, intercepted and daringly attacked a formation of sixty hostile land-based craft approaching our forces . . . shot down nine Japanese planes and completely disorganizing the enemy group, forced the remainder to abandon the attack before a single aircraft could reach the Fleet . . ."

And he kept score on his instrument panel with a pencil.

F6F Hellcat ▶

MITSUBISHI A6M5 *ZERO*

A Pacific dawn broke silently over Iwo Jima on 24 June 1944. The low overcast of a leaden sky was a welcome treat to the Japanese garrison manning the defenses of the tiny island. Their brief respite from the harassing American bombers and warships was to be short-lived, however. Almost immediately after 5 a.m. the familiar sounds of air raid warnings echoed over the island—a signal for the 80 defending *Zero* fighters to scramble and meet the attackers. Amid the klaxoning sirens they rose to swiftly form up tightly just beneath the overcast. The sky was void of Americans. On signal about half of the *Zeros,* led by veteran pilot Kinuste Moto, nosed up into the overcast. Breaking out into clear skies he found nothing. Then, suddenly bursting through the clouds, came a loose formation of Navy *Hellcats.* Immediately Moto attacked and in seconds had personally blasted four from the sky. Stunned by the surprise, the Americans throttled back into the cloud cover and on popping out ran headlong into the lower echelon of *Zeros* searching for them. Among these Japanese pilots was Saburo Sakai, an Ace in his own right. Sakai, during an earlier engagement, had lost his left eye which restricted his vision so vital in the fast-breaking situations of aerial warfare, especially dogfighting with superior machines such as the F6F. Nonetheless, Sakai and his group, assisted by the *Zeros* that had plunged back down from above the cloud cover, ripped into the American force and began separating it into easy "kill" segments. The *Hellcat* pilots, however, were fast to analyze the tactic and jumped to the offensive.

Saburo Sakai, strained by a long layoff from combat and hampered by his limited vision, broke off from the ensuing fast-paced action for a short breather before resuming the fight. Climbing back into the waning battle, Sakai slipped into position with what he surmised to be fifteen friendly *Zeros.* Closing on the group, he suddenly spotted the easily-recognized stars and bars on the *Hellcats.* Instinctively, he rolled away hoping they had not noticed his approach. Looking back, Sakai saw the *Hellcats* banking to the attack. Suddenly the impossible took place. Saburo found himself circling inside a wide circle of *Hellcats* whose pilots took turns breaking from the ring to attack him. Trying every evasive maneuver he had ever learned, none succeeded in shaking the *Hellcat* pilots, and his rolling dives that commenced at 1,600 feet suddenly put him on the deck. Ahead of him stood towering and dangerous cumulus cloud. Behind him were the *Hellcats.* Flying just above the waves (three times a wingtip cut a wave), Saburo raced headlong into the cumulus cloud. Tossed in every direction, the light *Zero* was suddenly thrust upside down into clear skies on the far side of the turmoil. Righting his plane, Saburo spotted the *Hellcats* regrouped on a course taking them away from Iwo.

A portion of the above-described action is captured on canvas, as Saburo makes his life-or-death high-speed escape run from hotly pursuing *Hellcat* pilots.

In this aerial engagement forty of Iwo Jima's eighty defending *Zeros* were shot down while the Americans lost ten *Hellcats,* a respectable 4:1 ratio. During the second engagement twenty additional *Zeros* fell to the guns of the powerful *Hellcats.* A third battle reduced the defending force by eleven more *Zeros,* leaving a token nine battle-weary fighters to defend Iwo Jima.

CHANCE-VOUGHT F4U
CORSAIR

During their desperate and futile bid to reverse the trend of action during the Battle of Leyte Gulf, the Japanese introduced to the Navy and the world a new word—*Kamikaze!*

Conceived out of necessity, the tactic was brutally simple. Faced with rapidly dwindling airpower (and virtually no experienced pilots), the Japanese could no longer mount the large scale aerial attacks that had once terrorized all areas of the Pacific and Southeast Asia. Instead of the conventional mass attack, it was now the lone fanatical *Kamikaze* pilot who flew his aircraft headlong through defending fighters and then heavy walls of flak to a suicidal death as he slammed into the largest warship he could see, usually a carrier.

Shortly after the introduction of the *Kamikaze* in late October, 1944, and before the invasion of Lingayen Gulf at Luzon in early January, 1945, the fast carrier *Essex* took on board the first carrier based *Corsairs* of the Marine Corps, VMF-124, and VMF-123.

Patrolling in the Sulu and China Seas, the *Essex's Corsairs* provided air support as the Americans took Mindoro Island, a stepping-stone enroute to Luzon, then began interrupting the enemy's attempts to beef-up their Lingayen Gulf defenses. In these seek-and-destroy missions what little Japanese air strength remained within striking distance of our invasion route and the Luzon objective was methodically searched out by the *Corsairs.* Not only were *Corsairs* seen in the Philippines but also over Formosa and Saigon. And so it was that during this time the *Kamikazes* of the Special Attack Corps found not only the *Essex* but also the *Cabot,*

Hancock and then, "Evil I," as the forever damaged *Intrepid* came to be known.

The scene is somewhere over the Philippines with *Corsairs* of VMF-124 breaking into a swarm of the suicide bent *Kamikazes*.

It would be an affront to this marvelous "bentwing" airplane and her many pilots and maintenance crews not to mention just how great the design really was. From a maiden flight in May of 1940, this powerful machine remained in "first-line" status until the 1960s, the longest service life of all fighters. As a propeller-driven craft the mighty *Corsair* outlived all other American-built fighters, land or carrier based.

GRUMMAN F8F *BEARCAT*

Bearcats brought to the table the best features of their older sisters, the F4F *Wildcats* and F6F *Hellcats,* plus a new power all their own.

Roughly the same size as the rugged *Wildcat* and possessing the protective armor of the deadly *Hellcat,* and with a magnificent powerplant, the F8F promised to be a winged hell in battle with the Japanese.

During February of 1945, *Bearcats* aboard the U.S.S. *Charger* pulled off carrier tests with excellent results.

In May the first *Bearcats* entered into service as VF–19. June and July saw the VF–19 brought up to strength (nearly fifty aircraft) while the squadron's pilots and crews underwent an exhaustive training program. Then, on 2 August the U.S.S. *Langley,* with VF–19 aboard, cast off all lines and headed for the far reaches of the western Pacific where the battle was raging ever closer to Japanese soil. Two destructive blasts at Nagasaki and Hiroshima gave the enemy a quick face-saving way out of the war. The *Langley* and her *Bearcats* of VF–19 never made it into action.

V–J Day did not, however, bring a halt to the F8F program as it did to so many others in progress. Production and pilot training of the *Bearcat* continued. In mid-1946 it was determined that F8Fs and F4Us would have to hold the line until the new jets could be brought into service. And it was about this time that the U.S. Navy selected the F8F to be the plane for their first "Blue Angels."

Came Korea in 1950 and the nod went to the F4U instead of the *Bearcat.* F4Us were known to be workhorses in support of the foot soldier. *Bearcats* were designed to be fighters. It appeared that the

Bearcat was destined to go the route of the monstrous B–36 and be denied the taste of battle.

Finally, on her third chance, the *Bearcat* got the call. She would fight in French colors and markings and right down on the deck where she had been denied the opportunity in Korea. The French in Indo-China, Vietnam in particular, used the F8F very effectively as a ground support aircraft even though the famous fight-to-the-finish stand at Dien Bien Phu was lost and brought an end to the French presence in that part of the world.

South Vietnam received the remaining French *Bearcats* when that country was separated from the North. Later, Thailand received F8Fs as a result of a U. S. Military Air Advisory Group program to strengthen that country's air power.

But all of that was long after this scene which catches a pair of *Langley* F8F *Bearcats* patrolling a naked Hawaiian sky in August of 1945—shortly before World War II closed its books.

◄ *F8F Bearcat*

NAKAJIMA Ki–43 *Oscar*
(Kamikaze)

The Japanese word *Kamikaze* means Divine Wind. Its signifi-
cance in Japanese history dates back to 1280 when the great Mon-
golian warlord, Kublai Khan, sent a huge invasion fleet to take the
Japanese islands. In a situation similar to that of the Spanish Armada in the English Channel, as the mighty Chinese naval force
lay off the Japanese coastline a killer typhoon moved in and
wrecked the fleet. To the Japanese this was indeed a *Kamikaze* sent
by the Sun Goddess to save them from certain annihilation. The
Divine Wind destroyed the Mongol naval threat and the Japanese
people survived.

Centuries later came the great Pacific war and the mighty United
States Navy. The two great sea powers tugged at one another until
the climax came at the Battle of Leyte Gulf. The Japanese Imperial
Navy moved into the Philippines in force to have it out with the
Americans, once and for all. The clash developed into a lop-sided
action with the U.S. Navy emerging as the clear-cut victor.

For some time prior to the Battle it had been recognized by some
Japanese naval officers that their air fighting effectiveness was all
but gone and in order to handle the powerful American fleets a
new and innovative tactic was needed. The answer lay in the suicide mission, where a 130-pound man in a single engine plane carrying a 500-pound bomb might be traded for a giant aircraft carrier
or cruiser. Thus, in 1944 the first *Kamikaze* Special Attack Corps
was formed and its pilots entered action for the first time during
the last days of the Battle of Leyte Gulf. And these *Kamikaze* attacks were successful. Emotions ran high among some Japanese
pilots to become a *Kamikaze*. They believed they would be as-

64

sured godhood at the Yakasuni Shrine if they gave their life for the emperor and country.

The successes at Leyte sent even greater numbers of the pilots into the action during the January 1945 invasion of Lingayen Gulf, and the *Kamikaze* attacks reached their peak during Operation "Iceberg," the invasion of Okinawa in April of 1945.

The once mighty Japanese Imperial Navy was now gone from the scene and with it practically all of her good first-line pilots. Japan faced an enemy armada of more than 1,500 ships that were knocking on the very doors of their homeland, a desperate situation not unlike what they had faced with the terrible Khan and his fleet. It rested with the *Kamikaze* pilots to destroy the American fleet. They were the only meaningful Japanese defense that remained.

The effectiveness of the *Kamikaze* was there; at least 40 American ships were sunk at Okinawa and more than 350 damaged. Had the tactic of *Kamikaze* missions been started earlier in the war, and been better organized, it would have delayed the United States timetable of events and caused the overall naval strategy to be reconsidered.

No ship was safe from the *Kamikaze,* but the aircraft carriers were the primary targets of the young pilots. The big U.S.S. *Franklin* fell victim during the Battle of Okinawa. Our painting shows another dedicated *Kamikaze* pilot driving his *Oscar* toward the burning, listing, but still fighting, warship. Will he make it to the fighting *Franklin,* will he be able to crash through the blistering firepower thrown up at him? When the action was over the *Franklin* counted some 700 dead and more than 250 wounded, and she was towed out of the battle by the cruiser *Pittsburgh.*

Heavy Bombers

BOEING B–17 *FLYING FORTRESS*

This tough "Queen's" battleground was anywhere the enemy elected to show himself. *Fortresses* will, however, always be remembered for their magnificent performance in disrupting the mighty Axis war machine. Massive daylight precision bombing attacks from high altitudes left Hitler's roofless European bastion in shambles. But that was later on. Before Hitler's legions would feel the might of the B–17 *Flying Fortresses* of General Ira Eaker's 8th Air Force, the rampaging Japanese would first have to face this aircraft in action.

On the third day after Pearl Harbor and after being all but decimated at Clark Field outside Manila, B–17 remnants of the 19th Bombardment Group made the first American aerial assault strike of the war when they bombed Japanese shipping near Vigan, Luzon.

After being whisked away from Corregidor and sped to Mindanao in PT boats, General MacArthur and his entourage continued the reluctant journey to Australia by B–17 *Flying Fortresses.*

It was from Australia that MacArthur would gather together what men and equipment he had, mold them into a fighting monster, and begin the long trek to Tokyo in consort with Admiral Nimitz. A part of MacArthur's seemingly-impossible task was the resurrection of a highly disorganized and demoralized air force.

Tales of unimaginable heroics and acts of great courage by B–17 airmen of "Blondy" Saunder's 11th Bombardment Group (H) during the time spent in containing the resolute Yamamoto, in his design for Australia and destruction of the U.S. Navy, are far too lengthy for an accounting here.

Selected to exemplify the courage and dedication of all *Fortressmen* and to refresh the memory of all as to the structural strength of this majestic airplane are a duo of 13th Air Force, 98th Squadron B–17Es, "Galloping Gus" and "Typhoon McGoon II," hooking it home after tearing up a piece of New Guinea real estate temporarily held by Japanese garrisons. Rising up to do battle with them are slow moving *Rufes,* easy marks for the *Fortresses* gunners. At the controls of "Typhoon McGoon" is Captain Walter Yates Lucas, Squadron Commander of the 98th.

March, 1943, was the beginning of the end of the *Fortress* presence in the Pacific. After fighting the decisive Battle of the Bismarck Sea, General Kenney (5th Air Force) went to Washington for the express purpose of getting more planes, especially B–17s. General Arnold denied his request for the B–17s and Kenney went straight to the president with the request. Again, he was told all B–17s were earmarked for Eaker's Eighth Air Force in Europe. Heavies in the Pacific were to be *Liberators* and the B–17's big sister, the gigantic B–29.

BOEING B–29 *SUPERFORTRESS*

The time is Wednesday the 23rd of May, 1945. Curtis LeMay's 20th Air Force B–29 *Superfortresses* are attacking the Japanese homeland again . . . this time the target is Tokyo's urban area. Four times previously Tokyo had been visited by the giant bombers that rained down fire and destruction. Tonight's mission (#181) and one more on the 25th of May (#183) are to be the final punches that will destroy most of Tokyo, reducing the area to a barren sea of ash.

Laboring northward from their four Marianas bases, 558 *Superfortresses* (the largest number of B–29s over a single target in WWII) from the 58th, 73rd, 313th and 314th Bomb Wings trudge for Japan; this long irregular chain of aluminum undulates gently under the glow from a three-quarter moon hanging in the southeastern sky. All eyes turn forward as the word is passed: *"Fuji . . . dead ahead!"* The familiar landmark looms in the distance, its majestic snow covered peak reflecting a dull red cast on the side facing Tokyo over fifty miles away, telling everyone that the pathfinders and lead bombers have made Tokyo a raging inferno.

Fuji is the signal to the crews to become even more alert. Ahead, only minutes away, they will make landfall, fix their position, then turn and take a new course for the run to target.

At least eighty-three attacks by enemy aircraft are made on the *Superforts* this night; the anti-aircraft fire is blistering hot, especially from Kawasaki and Yokohama to Tokyo. A seemingly endless corridor of searchlights spear the clouds, diffusing themselves to meld with the patterns cast by the fires of Tokyo. *Kamikazes* plow head-on into the armada of B–29s while *Betty* bombers

launch rocket powered *Baka Bombs* that blaze in from above the *Superfortresses;* most will take their one-way ride on a long, arching plunge to a collision on the ground or into the bay; a few however will connect and the sky is rent with pyrotechnics.

When it's all over two days later, Tokyo is stricken from the list as a target. More than fifty-six square miles of the city has been gutted by fire. All that remains upright are a few lucky smoke stacks and street light standards. The heavy stone bridges and paved streets are there, but all else in the target area is a barren waste.

Tokyo was one of sixty–five principal cities destroyed by the 20th Air Force. Five other great industrial areas were also reduced to rubble: Nagoya, Kobe, Osaka, Kawasaki, and Yokohama. The effect of the B–29 on Japan was overwhelming and certainly shortened the war and saved thousands, if not millions, of lives on both sides. The B–29 displaced an estimated 21,000,000 persons, and killed and wounded more than 800,000, which were more casualties than the combined Japanese armed forces suffered during the three and a half years of war with the United States.

Mission 181 was selected to portray the *Superfortresses.* In the foreground is the B–29 "Eddie Allen," a veteran of ten trips over the "Hump" and more than twenty missions against the enemy; Mission 181 was its seventh from the Marianas. This 58th Wing aircraft, a gift from the Boeing people, was named in memory of the Boeing test pilot who did much to develop and approve the B–17 and B–29, and who perished while trying to save the second B–29 prototype during a test flight in December 1942.

"Eddie Allen" has made its bomb run on Tokyo. Coming off target we see Captain Eino Jenstrom and his crew bank the mortally wounded aircraft away from the core of the huge Tokyo bonfire, away from the blinding lights and blastings of anti-aircraft bursts. Fire rages in the outer wing around the fuel cells where a dud round has slammed into the wing next to number one engine. This dud and the fire it caused will weaken the main spar structure and make the great airplane unsafe to fly again. This, then, is the final moments of the "Eddie Allen."

The "Eddie Allen" left an enviable combat record, as did virtually all *Superfortresses.* During eight months of combat, the big bomber hit targets in seven countries: Burma, Malaya, China, Manchuria, Formosa, Thailand, and Japan.

CONSOLIDATED B–24
LIBERATOR

At dawn on Sunday, the first day in August, 1943, 1,725 Americans in 178 bomb-laden B-24s rose from their airdromes in North Africa and began the assault that would be forever remembered by a single dynamic word, *PLOESTI!*

The stakes for Ploesti were high. The effort expended toward the destruction of the place was so great that this "Queen" of all *Liberator* actions produced five Medals of Honor.

Five Bomb Groups made the attack. One of these Groups was the 98th Pyramidiers which was led by the aggressive and audacious John R. "Killer" Kane. The Pyramidiers, with 47 severely weathered B–24's, drew the largest and most important target area in the Ploesti oil refinery complex—Astro Romana, code named "White Four."

For the assault on "White Four" Kane divided the Pyramidiers into five echelons, four composed of ten aircraft each and the fifth flying short with seven. Kane was centered in the first or leading flight and flew the lead position in John Young's *Liberator,* "Hail Columbia." Two planes away to his right was Lieutenant Royden LeBrecht piloting "The Squaw," the principal aircraft in the painting.

It was a long flight to Ploesti—better than six hours; plenty of time to let the mind recap all the courses and speeds and altitudes to target, more than enough time to mentally review that specific target site one more time. Halfway to target, Arens flying right wing to Kane, signals fuel troubles and aborts from the mission. LeBrecht moves "The Squaw" into the empty space beside "Hail Columbia."

Suddenly Ploesti explodes into life beneath the 98th with the slamming of rounds from German 88s being fired at point-blank ranges.

The situation worsens . . . rapidly. Another Group, Liberandos, miss a key turn coming off target and head into the on-rushing Pyramidiers roaring into Ploesti as planned. Walls of fire and mountains of heavy black smoke hide the specific targets so carefully memorized by the 98th's pilots. Kane, bearing down on all but obliterated Astro Romana, is faced with a crisis decision: continue or abort? He signals to continue the run to target. The 98th is met by steady anti-aircraft fire that is more intense and accurate than advised during briefing. The big bombers charge through the enemy's outer defenses then lunge past the on-coming Liberandos. Hurtling into the broiling inferno the lead pilots open up with their new nose-mounted 50 caliber machinegun clusters. A blossom of flame flashes from the bombers' noses and a fusillade of fifty caliber slugs blast a wide swath before them. Kane leads his ragged looking Pyramidiers into the boiling fireballs and thick oily smoke, past dangerous high-risen smoke stacks and by the menacing barrage balloon cables. After forever the bombs are finally released—and they explode prematurely for the low flying bomber crews. After spending an eternity of a few seconds in the hell of Astro Romana the 98th breaks into the clear on the far side of the furnace and begin to collect themselves for the sprint from the target area. The Pyramidiers come off target hurt, badly hurt, but behind them sprawls a blazing, bursting Astro Romana. "Tidal Wave," the code name for the overall assault on Ploesti, has done in the span-time of only a few precious moments what would have taken an Army of foot soldiers months and many dead to accomplish.

A new danger arises: "Hail Columbia's" number four engine feathered since run to target, shudders and slows speed . . . easy prey for a fighter. Kane quickly gathers in a couple more cripples (they are easy to find) and with the undamaged "Squaw" flying top cover to fend off any fighters takes a heading for the closest Allied airfield which is located at Nicosia, Cyprus. It is a long, long way from Ploesti to Nicosia when you are in an ailing B–24, and it would be dusk before the friendly island would come into view. But before Nicosia the little band would pass neutral Turkey, "Hadley's Harem" loses a pair of engines, signals goodbye, banks away and executes a perfect sea-ditching job next to the Turkish coastline below. "Hail Columbia" slows to near stall speed and the

battle weary trio of aircraft plod on toward Cyprus Island. As darkness settles around the *Liberators,* snuffing out the misery far behind them, Nicosia appears. LeBrecht piloting "The Squaw" and William Banks at the controls of the other *Liberator* land and make way for the in-coming badly damaged "Hail Columbia." Kane holds the big bomber on line with the runway and in the quickening darkness settles the aircraft down onto what he reckoned would be runway overage only to hit short, shear off all landing struts and crash land. Nobody was injured.

Ploesti took its toll on the rugged Pyramidiers. Most of the surviving B–24s suffered heavy battle damage and/or aircraft system malfunctions while only a few licked minor wounds. Only "The Squaw" came away from Ploesti without sustaining any battle damage or system failures; she was one of only three 98th Bomb Group aircraft that was on the line ready for a mission the day following Ploesti! This saucy little lady, named by Joe Kilgore, her first pilot, was due for a change in regard to battle damage . . . inside her empennage and waist sections remained the scars from more than two hundred bullet and cannon shot holes that Kilgore picked up from a dedicated Messerschmitt pilot during an earlier mission over Naples. In that action her tail turret and waist positions were shot away by the deadly accurate fighter. After 71 missions "The Squaw" had other scars, to be sure; but she had made it into and out of heavily fortified Ploesti without damage. In the end, "The Squaw's" and LeBrecht's crew were selected to return to the United States to participate in a War Bond Tour.

The part of the action selected to be portrayed was "The Squaw" and "Hail Columbia" as they blasted their way into Astro Romana. Here we have heavy bombers in the role of attack bombers and it isn't very often that you hear of heavies rigged with nose mounted machineguns. And the armorer mounted them with sections from bunk beds! This is one of the extremely rare occasions when pilots of heavy bombers actually had guns to fire.

Consolidated *Liberators* saw duty in all Theaters of Operations. The big burly bomber enjoyed the largest production run of any American made aircraft that saw service in World War II.

NORTH AMERICAN B–25
MITCHELL

If General MacArthur was to keep his famous promise "I shall return" to the people of the Philippines, then the Bismarck Barrier would first have to be broken.

Arching gently away from the northeast coast of New Guinea sits New Britain Island, the backbone of the Bismarck Barrier separating the Solomon and Bismarck Seas. Strategically situated on that island's northeast tip is Rabaul. With fine, deep-water port facilities, heavily protected by a ring of shore batteries, and no less than five excellent airfields nearby, Rabaul, the fortress, was the key to the Bismarcks.

As the "G.I." and Australians moved up the New Guinea coast from Buna-Gona and the Marines and sailors leap-frogged up the Solomons and Russells, General Kenney advanced his 5th Air Force bases even closer to the Bismarck Sea, New Britain, and Rabaul.

Rabaul, like Truk, her sister citadel in the Carolines, was destined to be by-passed by our invasion forces, but would be completely cleared of all air and naval power in the process.

There were many strikes carried out against Rabaul; the most bloody of all probably being that of 2 November 1943. Intelligence reported Simpson Harbor to be packed with ships. Kenney put nine B-25 Squadrons (all strafers) and six covering Squadrons of P–38 *Lightnings* into the air and headed them out for Rabaul. In addition to the existing massive anti-aircraft defenses guarding Rabaul, the B-25 crews also found heavily armed destroyers. In a strafing run, the pilots would have to bring their planes over Rabaul, bank toward the harbor area, drop down on the deck, and

come in fast, blazing away with all ten fifty caliber machine guns firing forward.

This one raid cost Kenney eight bombers, nine fighters and forty-five airmen, but Rabaul, would never quite be the same again. Rabaul itself blazed fiercely as tons of supplies, armament, fuel, and structures went up in smoke. In addition to more than thirty ships sunk or damaged, the enemy also lost nearly one hundred aircraft.

Coming at you in the painting is one of the eighty or so B–25 strafers tearing up Rabaul. Modified in the field by Major Paul I. "Pappy" Gunn, the B–25 "customized" into a strafer placed an enormous concentration of firepower up forward, four fifty calibers in the nose (he removed the bombardier's compartment and the lower turret) and two each mounted on both sides of the fuselage section just beneath the wing. And then there was the top turret gunner who could bring two more into forward firing position during the run to target.

This awesome amount of fire power when used in conjunction with the skip-bombing technique perfected by Kenney's B–25s and his own terror, the parafrags, broke the Bismarck and permitted MacArthur to hasten the pace along the northern New Guinea coast then back to the Philippines, where he did keep the promise.

DORNIER Do17

The *"Flying Pencil"!* And what a graceful shoulder-wing bomber was this twin-engine aircraft.

This gorgeous plane made her world debut in 1934. Like the Lockheed *Hudson* and Heinkel He III, the Do17 was originally designed for a civilian purpose. It was originally built to serve as a fast-flying mail carrier that also provided accommodations for six passengers. The first bomber version of the "Flying Pencil" appeared in 1936 and the bomber became operational the following year. In 1938 the Do17 was introduced into the Spanish Civil War fighting and gave an excellent account of itself in that action.

A large number of models were built of the Do17 with the final model being the Do17Z. It entered service in 1939. No other models appeared after the Do17Z.

The Dornier Do17 was a favorite bomber type of pilots and ground crews and the airplane was very reliable in the air. The bomber fell short in its capability to deliver the bigger payloads of its counterparts and as a result was phased out of the fighting in 1942, but not before giving a lusty account of herself.

Dornier Do17s were four-place aircraft and sported three 7.9mm MG 15 machineguns; one to the rear of the flight deck, another in the starboard side of the nose section and a third from the underside of the fuselage.

Dornier Do17s were used extensively by the Luftwaffe as support to Hitler's armies as they *blitzkrieged* Europe. During the Battle of Britain and "Operation Sealion," Hitler's grand design to take Britain, Do17s were used quite heavily, attacking shipping in the English Channel and hitting various targets in the British Isles.

Dorniers struck at Polish airfields and aircraft factories with high efficiency. After Poland there was a lull in the fighting, the "Phony War" of the winter of 1939–1940, as all sides took a breather and re-grouped. During this lull Do17s paid regular visits over France and dropped leaflets and took photographs but released no bombs. Then in May of 1940 the real war was started when the Germans blitzed into Holland, Belgium and Luxembourg. On that day in May the commanding officer of *Groupe de Chasse* 1/5, a part of the famous "Stork Wing," was flying patrol from his airfield at Suippes and he encountered five Do17s over Mourmelon at 12,000 feet. Capitaine Jean Accart engaged the Dorniers and one was shot down and the remainder turned away from the action. Later in the day the French flown Curtiss 75A *Hawks* encountered 21 more Do17s striking at Suippes and their airfield and shot down several and dispatched the rest.

The action portrayed is the *Hawks* engaging the graceful Do17.

Dornier Do17 ▶

Attack Aircraft

JUNKERS JU87 *STUKA*

The *Stuka,* like the famous sharkmouth P–40s, is legend in the annals of aviation history. *Stuka* is an abbreviation of the German word *Sturzkampfflugzeug* which when translated means literally "dive-bomber." The design broke onto the world scene in the early 1930s and first tasted combat during the Spanish Civil War in the late '30s, and the airplane was highly effective in that action.

When Hitler unleashed the infamous *blitzkrieg* on Poland the first of September 1939, the ugly, bird-like *Stukas* hurled their fury unmercifully on the Polish defenders. Unopposed the *Stukas* screamed down onto bridge sites, factories and the great city of Warsaw to bring the fear of death wherever they attacked.

After Poland came the conquest of the Low Countries, Holland, Belgium and Luxemborg, and the terrorizing and deadly accurate *Stuka* was again in consort with the lightning fast German army. Fighting again, unopposed in the skies, the *Stukas* added to their terrifying reputation of being the carrier of great fear, death and destruction. It was an honest assessment! The aircraft's vulnerability began to show itself, however, in subsequent actions over France where the Curtiss *Hawk* 75s were able to badly maul unescorted Junkers JU87s.

And when the German noose closed on Dunkirk, Luftwaffe *Stukas* were sent in to demolish the shipping that had come to rescue the retreating Allied soldiers. It was here that the beginning of the end for the terrible *Stuka* took place as defending *Hurricane* and *Spitfire* pilots ripped the dive-bombers to pieces.

It was the Battle of Britain that rang down the curtain for the JU87; the craft simply could not be defended when up against

Spitfires and Hurricanes, and any German fighter escort advantages were lost the instant the *Stukas* began their dives. The airplane was exceptionally vulnerable right after bomb release, during the pull-up. The resulting *G* forces usually blacked-out the crew and left the airplane defenseless for a moment after the action.

While the Junkers JU87 really lost its terror during the Battle of Britain, operational use of the aircraft continued on all fronts right up to the end of hostilities.

Probably one of the most famous of all *Stuka* pilots is Hans Ulrich Rudel, portrayed here as he lines up on yet another Russian tank. It is said that he participated in excess of 2,500 missions and attacked practically every kind of target. Among Rudel's victims were the Russian battleship *Marat,* which he sank with a 2,200 pound bomb placed on target from a 90 degree angle of attack, and more than 500 enemy tanks.

DOUGLAS A–20 *HAVOC*
(BOSTON)

Douglas A–20 *Havocs* were the main attack bomber of the Army Air Corps when America entered the war. It was an extremely popular aircraft and ultimately flew combat missions in all theaters of war and in the colors and markings of many of the Allied nations.

The French were early importers of the *Havoc,* the export version labeled DB–7. It was this sleek aircraft that prowled the North African battlegrounds of Tunisia with French crews from Squadron 15 out of Youks-les-Bains. These *Bostons* (as the *Havocs* were called when exported) fought the elite Afrika Korps all over Tunisia. They were everywhere, ripping into German tanks, hugging the hot desert sands as they roared in to mangle General Rommel's well-camouflaged field artillery positions, bursting out of nowhere to disrupt advancing convoys, keeping storage and supply depots in a constant state of confusion and disrepair, and making life miserable for Axis shipping, usually secondary but delightful targets.

Before 1942 was out the U.S. Army Corps 47th Bomb Group arrived from the States with original order Douglas A–20 *Havocs* and took over the 15th's remaining battered DB–7 *Bostons.* From then on the 47th flew support for the U.S. II Corps and hit German targets mainly in central Tunisia, Sfax, Gabes and along the Mareth Line.

In the painting are three 47th Bomb Group *Havocs* attacking shipping running out of Sfax harbor.

94

DOUGLAS SBD *DAUNTLESS*

While this painting deals strictly with elements of Lieutenant Commander Clarence W. McClusky's eighteen SBDs from the U.S.S. *Enterprise* as they plunge from 17,000 feet to pulverize the heavy carrier *Soryu*, an appreciation of the Battle of Midway would slip by if the reader were not aware of some supporting information. A brief look at the differential in the strength of the opposing forces is both revealing and astonishing.

Yamamoto, the architect of the Japanese adventure at Pearl Harbor, was also the designer of the Midway action. And he was nobody's fool. His strength included eight carriers (four heavy class), eleven battleships, a mixture of twenty-two light and heavy cruisers, more than sixty destroyers and in excess of twenty submarines—a formidable force of warships in anybody's Navy. In addition, at least 700 aircraft consisting of dive-bombers, fighters and torpedo bombers were at his disposal. In their cockpits sat a respectable number of highly seasoned, battle-wise, first-line pilots. And topping it all off was the fact that Yamamoto was the most brilliant naval strategist/tactician produced by Japan in modern times.

Pitted against this vast array of sea power was Rear Admiral Fletcher's relatively inferior force. It consisted of three carriers (one of which, the *Yorktown,* had been hastily repaired at Pearl after sustaining damage during earlier bloodletting in the Coral Sea action), one light cruiser, seven heavy cruisers and fifteen destroyers. And he could put into the air some 230 aircraft from his carriers and cruisers plus an assortment of navy and marine combat aircraft, based on Midway, that totalled slightly under 100. Then

95

there were the seventeen Army Air Corps B–17s from Hawaii and the four B–26 *Marauders* converted into torpedo bombers. Anyway you figured it, the numerical odds definitely favored Yamamoto.

Yamamoto divided his forces into three groups—one to move north and attack the Aleutian Islands off Alaska, the second to attack Midway, while the third, from where he would direct the battle, maneuvered well out of the fighting arena but close enough to move in when the American Navy showed itself.

His intended objective in sending a force north to the Aleutians was to draw out into the open the remnants of the U.S. fleet. It was determined the Americans would surely move to vigorously oppose any offense made against their territory, regardless of its geographical location. Concurrent with this part of the strategy, Admiral Nagumo's 1st Carrier Force would drive hard for Midway. Fortunately, early in the morning of 3 June 1942, a lone PBY spotted Nagumo's force moving toward Midway.

Mid-morning on the 4th of June, McCluskey led his sixty-one aircraft (thirty-seven SBDs) from the U.S.S. *Enterprise* to seek out Nagumo's carriers. A similar force from the *Hornet* was launched. Fletcher, aboard the *Yorktown,* committed thirty-five more to the offensive flight. After great frustration in searching for an elusive enemy, aircraft from the *Hornet* spotted half of Nagumo's carrier force and sped to the attack. Almost immediately torpedo bombers from *Enterprise* and *Yorktown* dashed for the other half that they had spotted. Of the forty-one planes that attacked thirty-five were destroyed by *Zeros* that swooped down from above or by deadly accurate anti-aircraft fire from the carriers and their escorts. Carrier defense against the torpedo planes was so effective that not a single torpedo scored a hit.

The sacrifice, however, was quickly and thoroughly avenged. The carrier's protective screen of *Zeros* that had gone to the deck to maul the torpedo bombers had left the skies clear for the SBDs. *Dauntlesses* from *Hornet* and *Yorktown* selected *Kaga* while McClusky divided his *Dauntlesses* into two formations and hit *Soryu* and *Akagi.* The fourth carrier, *Hiryu,* was far north of the action and was left alone until later in the evening when *Dauntlesses* from *Enterprise* laid four solid hits on her flight deck.

By the morning of 5 June, all four carriers of Nagumo's 1st Carrier Force had been sunk along with several ships of the line. The Japanese Imperial Fleet had suffered its first defeat in 300 years.

Of the thirty-six aircraft depicted in this gallery of paintings, no less than eight types were actively engaged in the fighting at Midway, the PBY *Catalina,* SBD *Dauntless,* F4F *Wildcat,* B–17 *Flying Fortress,* B–26 *Marauder,* TBF *Avenger* and the *Zero.*

Yamamoto's diversionary force in the north yielded nothing for him. It did, however, give the Americans one crash-landed *Zero* in excellent condition. Flight tests of this airplane were instrumental in developing its nemesis, the F6F *Hellcat.*

DOUGLAS A–26 *INVADER*

With the Battle of the Bulge behind them, the Allies once again began moving the irregular-shaped battle lines to an increasing shorter length as positions were firmly stabilized, and the noose was drawn tighter and tighter around Nazi Germany. The end of Nazism would come on 7 May 1945, but not before a reluctant enemy made his last ditch stands.

By the 21st day of April, seventeen brutal days and nights before a silence would descend on the larger part of Europe, the once powerful Luftwaffe had seen its Wagnerian "dawn of the gods" fade from existence. Allied airpower struck hard at targets that gave back little opposition. The earlier "Operation Clarion," a concentrated effort of interdiction in which the fire-breathing A–26s inflicted burning waste on the German communication and supply systems, had been highly effective. Then, "Operation Grenade," which came immediately on the heels of "Clarion," saw the A–26s chewing up German armor in front of the advancing Allied foot soldiers in their drive to the Rhine.

As the noose closed on Germany, the 9th Air Force's mediums, which included the fearsome *Invaders,* intensified their roles of interdiction, always a few steps ahead of our racing armies routing the badly beaten emeny that had once invaded, then subjugated, no less than fifteen nations. As freedom came to these nations, their people swarmed into the streets welcoming and greeting their liberators. And overhead, hurtling to the next concentration of Germans making their last stand were the deadly A–26 *Invaders* of the 9th Air Force.

On the 21st day of April in 1945, the 386th, 391st, and 416th

Bomb Groups of the 9th Air Force (all flying the slender A–26s), along with Douglas A–20s of the 410th, flew in excess of 120 interdiction sorties to raze the railroad marshalling yard at Attnanpucheim in Austria. The low flying bombers caused tremendous damage, witnessed no flak at all, and lost not a single aircraft as they also cut the main line from Vienna to southern Germany.

Bottled up in a small pocket of western Germany were the remaining seasoned troops of Germany. They would go nowhere! On the 28th of April, only a few days after the massive interdiction raid on Attnanpucheim, nattily uniformed Germans entered the Allied Headquarters located in the ancient palace of the kings of Naples at Caserta, Italy, and began dickering for surrender terms.

By the 1st of May, only eleven days after the raid on Attnanpucheim, the word would be out that Hitler was dead.

One by one the death dealing rattle of the *Invader's* guns fell silent, and their crews slipped the racy bombers into landing patterns for the last time.

It is noteworthy that while the A–26 only managed a beginner's track record during World War II, it was a good one—so good, in fact, that the craft was resurrected many years later to tear up the Ho Chi Minh Trail wandering down from the north into South Vietnam.

CURTISS SB2C *HELLDIVER*

The Battle of Leyte Gulf is considered to have commenced on 23 October 1944, and to have ended on the 26th. Because of the sheer numbers of warships and aircraft involved and the sprawling expanse of territory over which the battle took place, the action is justified in being remembered as the greatest sea battle of all times.

As in practically all other Pacific engagements of any magnitude, it was the airplane that made the difference. It was here during the waning hours of battle that the Japanese effectively introduced the *Kamikaze.*

Many months prior to Leyte, the Japanese had developed a master strategy plan code-named Operation *Sho; Sho* meaning Victory. Operation *Sho* considered four offensive actions to be taken by the Allies, one of which, *Sho–1,* concerned the Philippines. In countering an offensive in the Philippines, *Sho–1* would, and did, bring practically all remaining naval and air power of the Japanese into the action; it was a pincer movement from north and south complemented by a diversionary force to draw U.S. carriers and planes away from the main battle site. And so it was that Admiral Halsey, Commander-in-Chief of the 3rd Fleet, was sucked in. He raced north into the Philippine Sea to have it out once and for all with what he considered to be the main attacking force of the Japanese. Halsey took more than sixty warships and 750 aircraft into an engagement against Vice-Admiral Ozawa's seventeen warships carrying a meager thirty aircraft, the decoy force of *Sho–1.*

Needless to say, Halsey's tremendous advantage tore Ozawa's force apart, sinking all four of his carriers, a cruiser plus destroyers, and downing every one of the aircraft. On the 25th of October

elements of the 3rd Fleet were only forty miles from Ozawa's fleeing, battered force when orders from Nimitz turned the bulk of Halsey's forces southward to enter the fierce fighting that was raging near Leyte Gulf.

Helldivers played a major role in turning *Operation Sho–1* into a disaster for the enemy. Never again would the once mighty Japanese Imperial Fleet pose a threat to the advancing Allies.

On 26 October it was all over, but not before this *Helldiver* pilot from the U.S.S. *Hancock,* a part of Task Group 38.1 left behind by Halsey to finish off Ozawa, selects one of the scattering remnants of the decoy force as his target and drops down for the kill.

The *Helldiver,* or "Big-tailed Beast" as the aircraft was frequently called, was the last design in a long line of pure dive bombers built by America. Plagued by a host of design changes, the big craft was late in making her appearance with the fleet in the Pacific; however, she replaced the tired but steady *Dauntless* in time for the Battle of the Philippine Sea.

GRUMMAN TBF *AVENGER*

Grumman-designed and built TBF *Avengers* entered the Pacific war in early June, 1942, just in time to make their fighting debut in the Battle of Midway.

Assigned to operate from the U.S.S. *Hornet* with Torpedo Squadron 8, TBFs were aboard the carrier with six held in reserve, land-based on Midway Island.

It was these six reserve *Avengers* of Torpedo Squadron 8 that were committed to the fighting on the first day, and it was these *Avenger* pilots who made first contact with the enemy. As they streaked in fast and low for the carriers, swarms of screening *Zeros* dropped down onto them. Breaking through the *Zeros,* the remaining *Avengers* were met by a wall of blistering anti-aircraft fire from the enemy warships. Not only was the flak heavy, deadly, and accurate; but shells exploding in the water ahead of the torpedo planes threw up pillars of water equally as dangerous as the gunfire.

The heroism of Torpedo Squadron 8 is reflected here as we see Lieutenant A.K. Bert Earnest piloting *Avenger* 8–T–1, the only surviving aircraft of Torpedo 8, through withering fire as he hurtles toward his target, the Japanese carrier *Akagi.*

On the second day of battle the remaining aircraft of Torpedo 8 were committed to action from the deck of the *Hornet.* None returned.

Although thoroughly mauled at Midway, the big *Avengers* bounced back to be a continual menace to the Japanese. Among the more prominent victims to fall before the *Avengers* were the two Japanese super-battleships, *Musashi* and *Yamato.* In late October,

105

1944, *Avenger* pilots caught *Musashi* out of Singapore enroute to participate in the Battle of Leyte Gulf and sent her to the bottom with three solid hits. *Yamato* met a similar fate in April of 1945 as she tried in vain to break up the invasion of Okinawa.

It is interesting to note that *Avengers* went on to play important peace-time roles as civilians after the war. A redesigned bomb bay made the huge plane exceptionally adaptable as a forest fire water bomber machine.

DE HAVILLAND *MOSQUITO*

Launched by British Air Marshal A. T. "Bomber" Harris, the first 1,000 bomber plane raid, dubbed "Operation Millennium," completely overwhelmed the Rhine River city of Cologne, Germany, the night of 30 May 1942. The resulting devastation was but a prelude to what was to become a recurring nightmare for the Germans.

The Air Marshall left no psychological stone unturned. In the early morning hours following his first "Millennium," a new sound descended upon Cologne when four speedy *Mosquitoes* scattered Germans busily engaged in cleaning up the damage from the earlier massive raid.

Eventually "Mossies" became highly specialized in this kind of follow-up operation, moving in quickly behind heavy bombardments with a couple of "block-buster" bombs, then returning home at high speed. Although they were capable of being heavily armed, Mossies usually flew pathfinding missions (spotting the target area for the following heavy bombers) and nuisance raids completely unarmed. With the lightened load, the twin-engined craft were so fast that the best the Luftwaffe could put in the air rarely caught a "Mossie." This tremendously effective aircraft enjoyed the lowest loss rate of any aircraft within Bomber Command.

It is significant that the tactical performance and design of this plane had such an impact on Hitler that it was instrumental in delaying the production of the twin-jet Messerschmitt Me262 for an entire year so it could undergo redesign to parallel more closely the fighter-bomber configuration of the *Mosquito.* This interruption of the Me262 program possibly denied the Luftwaffe a potential aerial warfare superiority that undoubtedly would have altered the course of the war.

In the early morning of 11 April 1944, Wing Commander R. H. Bateson of No. 613 Squadron led six *Mosquitoes* fast and low over Holland. His objective? The five story Gestapo Headquarters across from the Peace Palace at The Hague. Here we see two of those six *Mosquitoes* just after they have neatly bounced a pair of bombs through the front door of the Gestapo building.

AICHI TYPE 99 D3A1 *(VAL)*

This first-line Japanese dive-bomber was first introduced to action during the China fighting. The Aichi Type 99 went on to become a menace to Allied fleet elements in the Indian and Pacific oceans.

Val dive-bomber pilots were among the best in the world, a result of intensive training. Their proficiency in dive-bombing techniques gave them a fantastic "direct hit rate" of 82 percent effectiveness during naval action in the Indian ocean.

Val dive-bombers were in the action all the way. At Pearl Harbor there were 51 Aichi Type 99 aircraft in the first strike group led by Flight Lieutenant Kakuichi Takahashi. These first strike dive-bombers scored heavily on the sleeping U.S. Navy and Army Air Corps. The second assault group entered the Pearl Harbor action at 9:00 A.M. and 80 *Vals* finished off the job started by the earlier strike group.

As the war moved closer to the homeland islands it was the trusty Aichi Type 99 that saw extensive use during the *Kamikaze* actions.

The craft was so versatile that on occasions it doubled as a fighter.

In the action depicted we see a *Val* off the carrier *Soryu* as its pilot lines up on a Pearl Harbor target.

112

Patrol Bombers

LOCKHEED *HUDSON*

What a machine this lovely lady was. War was not her "thing," but the far-sighted British knew a good bomber when they saw one.

A product of Lockheed ingenuity during the middle 1930s, *Hudsons* (as the British would come to call them) were designed to compete with Douglas DC–2/3 type aircraft. Lockheed's plane was shoved into the world's limelight in 1938 when young Howard Hughes circled the globe in one, taking only three days, nineteen hours and eleven minutes.

British aircraft purchasers in this country asked Lockheed to give them a proposal covering a bomber version of the plane because they liked what they had seen of the aircraft's performance, and Lockheed could obviously turn them out in acceptable quantities. Most important, however, was the speed of the big, ruggedly build Lockheed airplane. It was faster than anything the British had in their inventory.

Lockheed's bomber-version proposal was accepted, and deliveries of *Hudsons* began shortly before Hitler's attack on Poland brought France and Britain into the war.

Almost immediately German U-boats began raiding British bound convoys, sinking ships loaded with the badly needed *Hudsons.* The plea went out to begin ferrying them by air across the wild Atlantic, and overnight the losses of *Hudsons* dropped significantly.

Hudsons quickly became the mainstay of the Coastal Command and were rated in popularity by the Britishers as second only to their magnificent Supermarine *Spitfire.*

115

Every plane has its great moment of glory. For the sturdy *Hudson* it was Dunkirk. Like mother hens guarding their flocks, the *Hudson* pilots gave unceasing support to the bloodied British soldiers who had managed to make it to the beaches at Dunkirk.

More than two hundred German U-boats were sunk by *Hudsons;* countless others were damaged, and one was even captured by a 269th Squadron *Hudson* one August morning in 1941. Damaged to such a degree that it could not submerge, the German gun crews swung into action against the *Hudson* only to be shot to pieces. Each time the U-boat skipper put another gun crew to work, the *Hudson's* guns would down them with blistering return fire. Unable to submerge or fight, the skipper could only give up.

Hudson armament varied, especially as time wore on. In its earlier actions, however, it sported five 30-caliber machine guns, two in the Boulton-Paul top turret (which, incidently was installed in Britain rather than during production stateside), two in the nose section mounted in a fixed position above the bombardier and one belly gun.

The USAAF designation of the *Hudson* was A–28 Attack Bomber while the Navy designated it PBO–1 Patrol Bomber.

Here we look down on a familiar *Hudson* pastime, catching a German U-boat running on the surface. A pair of them from the Coastal Command begin the deadly act of destroying it.

CONSOLIDATED PBY
CATALINA

Somewhere in the middle of the Coral Sea a *Catalina* begins cranking down its wingtips preparatory to making a landing in moderate seas. Two more airmen will be saved to fight again.

Tales of the venerable PBY are too bountiful even to begin to relate here. Many action-packed scenes of daring, victory and tragedy remain to be painted about this slow moving, low-flying, long-range flying boat that enjoyed the largest production run of any flying boat in history.

In addition to a formidable array of machine guns, the *Catalina* (named by the British and adopted by the U.S.) could prowl the sea lanes carrying four depth charges, or up to four thousand pounds of bombs or a couple of torpedoes mounted beneath the huge wings.

Strong construction permitted the PBY to absorb great punishment by heavy seas or eager enemy fighter pilots. While plenty of "May Day" victims owe their lives to the air-sea rescue ability of the "Cats" or "Dumbos," as the great craft were fondly called, the enemy also had a healthy respect for its other versatile uses. In May of 1941, an R.A.F. Coastal Command PBY shadowed the mighty German battleship, *Bismarck*, as it broke out of the Baltic. *Catalinas* found the Japanese Midway Invasion force and then later were the first to attack, thereby opening the Battle of Midway. The last to leave Manila Bay and little Corregidor, the island symbol of a national pride, were a pair of PBY *Catalinas*. Coastal Command *Catalinas* posed a continuous threat to German U-boat crews, and more than one U-boat fell prey to the Royal Canadian

Air Forces "Cansos," the name given to the PBY by our Allies to the north.

By some estimations more than one hundred PBY's still roam the skies today, a fine testimonial to a great plane who had its maiden flight way back in March of 1935!

Scout and Liaison Aircraft

VOUGHT–SIKORSKY OS2U
KINGFISHER

Kingfishers were in the action all the way, from the attack on Pearl Harbor to the "signing" on the decks of the *Missouri.* In between these two momentuous events the rugged OS2U served the fleet in numerous capacities but predominately as "eyes" for the big guns of the battleships and cruisers and for rescue work.

It is the latter that we selected to present the OS2U *Kingfisher.* The people of Yaptown, Yap Island in the Carolines, basked in a pleasant, typical Pacific morning sun on the 27th of July 1944. The big harbor was peaceful; only an occasional whitecap broke the monotony of its surface. Overhead were scattered, fluffy cumulus clouds, cotton-balls hanging listlessly in the rich blue sky. Then, Task Force 58 with its 125 ships of the line (sixteen carriers) struck from fifty miles away. Around mid-day *Avengers* and *Hellcats* of VT–31 and VF–31 from the carrier *Cabot* struck Yaptown from the inland side of the city. The *Avengers,* each armed with four 100 pound general purpose bombs, made their bomb runs from 15,000 feet dropping down over the target then levelling off at 500 feet as they raced out over the harbor.

In mid-run to target a TBM of VT–31 is hit in the main fuel tank by flak. The pilot drops his bombs. The cockpit is burning. Still he holds the big ship at 500 feet until his two crewmen finally clear their aft compartment, which is also burning. Only then does the pilot leave the burning aircraft. Three are burned and down in the harbor. The enemy shore installations begin firing on them, but the shots pass overhead. The guns cannot be depressed low enough to get them, and the three are just beyond the range of smaller weapons. While VF–31 *Hellcats* go to work strafing the shore batteries, a

123

call is flashed to the anti-sub patrol for a *Kingfisher*.

Within minutes a *Kingfisher* from the cruiser *Columbia* was on the scene, its pilot bringing the aircraft in low and straight for the wounded *Avenger* crewmen. Now the shore batteries took him on as a target. The water came alive from exploding shells, still the OS2U came on to the men. After loading the TBM's pilot into the rear seat, his two crewmen sat on the wings and held on. The OS2U pilot would now dash over the water for the pick-up submarine five miles away. On the way out the *Kingfisher* pilot must pass through the entire effective range of the guns on the beach— and it is this section of the action that you see in the painting.

The end of the story is that thanks to a *Kingfisher* and her pilot and radioman-gunner, three more American lives were saved. After the long taxi to the submarine, the two *Avenger*-enlisted crew members were transferred. Then, with the *Avenger* pilot still snuggled down in the rear seat and its usual occupant setting astride the fuselage just behind him, the OS2U pilot took off for a rendezvous with the *Columbia*.

STINSON L–5 *SENTINEL*

What do you do when the mission is to hit Madang during mid-morning and you find them hitting back? On a bad day you might feel that unmistakable shudder ripple through your rugged A–20 and know you have taken a bad hit. The gauges get around to verifying your suspicions. The starboard engine growls into a twisted mess. Flames slice over the wing, an omnious prelude to a fatal explosion. The entire empennage shakes so violently that you wonder what is holding it all together.

It has all happened so fast that you are a healthy fifteen miles downwind before you know it. Your altitude is slightly above tree-top level. Then, as if God willed it, ahead of you manifests a patch of lovely Kunai grass. Everything is either feathered or shut down. The word is hastily passed to prepare for an unscheduled landing. Flaps down full, nose up, gear up, fingers crossed, you let her down. Perfect! You've temporarily ruined a swath of the plush eight- to twelve-foot-high Kunai grass, but not one additional wrinkle was put in the plane as you sat her down.

Worried? Not particularly! A Jap patrol, having seen the masterful aerial demonstration, might saunter in for depositions and then take you on a nasty hike; or hungry *Zeros, Rufes,* or *Franks* could happen by looking for a helpless statistic, but more likely the beautiful red and white striped tail of an all silver 25th Liason Squadron L–5 *Sentinel* would "mosey" by to assess the situation. It's the Guinea Short Lines at work, dedicated for some mystical reason to pull off the impossible, if only to satisfy themselves.

Getting down is one thing; getting back up is quite another. Like yourself, the L–5 pilots can ease into the high, cushioning Kunai.

Getting out is the problem. Everyone goes to work hacking down the Kunai transforming it into a makeshift runway. After an enormous amount of effort, it's time to try. Four-hundred pounds is the L–5's gross load limit according to the unused tech order. You weigh a solid 175. The pilot is a definite 160. Lots to spare! You case your lanky co-pilot and overweight gunner, then almost choke when the L–5 pilot decides on the gunner. Reluctantly you sit in your gunner's lap and look over the L–5 driver's shoulders. Ahead of you is a nasty tree line that rises frightfully high. Way overweight, a short makeshift runway . . . everyone sweats a little. It's now or never. Grinning, the sergeant pilot sets the brakes and revs it up until the wings are about to shake off. Just when the whole thing seems ready to disintegrate, he releases the brakes and the L–5 lurches forward. The trees loom up ahead. Death seems imminent. A miracle occurs as the wheels leave the stubble. The trees are taller than ever. To climb over them is aerodynamically impossible. Without giving the impending catastrophe a second thought, the sergeant pilot makes a squeaky left bank. Completely rigid, you watch as (nobody will believe this) he calmly threads his way through the jungle gaining altitude at every opportunity. Dumbfounded, you suddenly become aware that he has broken out of the tree line and into blue sky. You breathe again and wonder if all those promises to God will be kept.

It is all in a day's work for the unheralded men of the Guinea Short Lines, really the 25th Liason Squadron. They gained the title for getting you from your downed position back to home base in the most direct line; hence, Short Lines. Their feats are legend. Some of their stories are so bizarre that only those airmen involved would believe them.

This selected scene portrays the most common mission/task confronting the 25th. It speaks fairly well for what it was all about.

MESSERSCHMITT Bf 108b
TAIFUN

Had Willi Messerschmitt, the great German aircraft designer, been a less dedicated man in his advance thinking, the mainstay of the Luftwaffe, the dreaded Bf 109, would have never existed.

The year was 1934, the middle of a world depression and the rising tide of Nazism. Willi chose this time to unveil the most remarkable aircraft design ever seen in the sports field—the Messerschmitt Bf 108a. The design received immediate and wide acclaim, and offers began to come in from outside Germany.

Quick on the heels of these orders came the feared Gestapo. Willi's simple logic caused second thoughts in certain quarters of the German hierarchy: "In the absence of local support he was forced to design and sell to foreign markets."

Professor Messerschmitt was permitted to enter the 1935 fighter design competition and almost immediately faced the obstacle designed to bankrupt his operations. While all other competitors were to receive German made engines (compliments of the government), *none* were available to Messerschmitt.

Willi's design was not only simple but extremely functional and, as it turned out, flexible. Going with what he had in the 108 design, he reduced the girth for four passengers down to a sleek one that would accommodate a lone pilot. This, in turn, allowed a lengthening of the fuselage which was necessary to house a more powerful engine, accessories, armament and larger fuel tanks. However, the 108 nose, wings, and tail section remained remarkably the same in appearance in the new 109 configuration. And Messerschmitt solved the riddle of the engine problem by incorporating a less powerful but satisfactory British Rolls-Royce Kestrel V en-

gine, the same powerplant that would be pitted against the Bf 109 in later years inside England's Supermarine *Spitfires*.

The highly modified 108 and its British powerplant lost out to Heinkel in the competition trials. However, Willi's 109 gave good enough account of itself that the fledgling Messerschmitt organization received an order for ten production models. The rest is history. At last count in excess of 33,000 Bf 109s were manufactured in a multitude of variants and by many European firms, the longest production run of any aircraft in history. And it all began with the radical design of the Bf 108a.

During the war years Messerschmitt's Bf 108bs were built in limited quantities to serve as liaison and courier duty aircraft. Such is the scene depicted here; a *Taifun* pilot gives his passengers a look at Castle Neuschwanstein as he threads his way through the Bavarian Alps enroute to the Black Forest from Salzburg.

MISSING MAN FORMATION

Long recognized within the flying community as the highest honor that can be bestowed upon those airmen who made the supreme sacrifice in the defense of their country is the solemn heart-rending tribute known by airmen the world over as the *Missing Man Formation.*

It signifies that a pilot or crew for reasons beyond their control cannot fly and fill the formation. The *Missing Man Formation* is usually executed at low level, about sunset, and is composed of either four or five aircraft that do not all have to be of the same type.

For this formation and scene five aircraft were used, all of which are F4F *Wildcats* of VMF–211, the Marine Fighter Squadron destined to fly into history during their courageous stand at lonely Wake Island in late 1941. It was a desperate but futile battle of which there would be no surviving aircraft. Helplessly, the U.S. Navy and A.A.F. sat by and died a thousand deaths as the tiny fortress fought back with all the heart and soul possessed by men. Absolutely vulnerable to the guns of the Japanese warships and the overwhelming numbers of aircraft types that would be launched against them, the Marines of Wake Island preferred to fight to the end rather than take the easy way out and surrender without putting up a fight. Major Devereaux commanded all of Wake, its 478 tough marines, their few batteries of five and three inchers plus twelve *Wildcats,* four of which were operational most of the time.

Nonetheless, they held the line from 7 December 1941 to 22 December when the Japanese landed an overpowering force and shot

down the last two remaining F4Fs but not before the pilots had sunk an enemy destroyer.

The loss of these courageous fighting Marines and the entire force of VMF–211 exemplifies the discipline and determination of the U. S. Marine wherever he is found. It is only fitting that the *Missing Man Formation* saluting all missing airmen should be composed of VMF–211 *Wildcats* off Wake Island.

EPILOGUE

So, where did they all go; the aircraft and the warriors, those who fought *and* those who built? It is a question, a subject, that is very rarely mentioned even in a passing way. We simply never give their final disposition another thought. It was a bad dream that is now behind us and we are prone to forget such things as quickly as possible . . . it is impossible to "recall" pain.

We all remember it was a fight to the finish . . . no compromising. And that is decidedly how it was concluded. Part and parcel of the surrender terms was the total destruction of the enemies' capacity to build instruments of war. This included the demolition of *all* flight items save a precious few destined for engineering study. The back of the remnants of the Axis aerial might was summarily broken . . . forever.

This demolition was not limited to the Axis powers alone, however. Ramps of new A–26 *Invaders* were rendered useless by dynamite on their European bases. Thousands of B–24 *Liberators* were destroyed on tiny Biak Island, New Guinea, and left for the jungle to consume them.

And so it went around the world. The order of the day seemed to be to render useless all but a precious few, guardians of the peace. At home the destruction was even more pronounced. Here we had the great smelters, the fiery furnaces that could in the twinkling of an eye reduce a spanking brand new B–17 or sleek P–51 into a batch of gleaming aluminum ingots. Arizona in particular became the national graveyard for all these majestic, freedom-saving aircraft. The furnaces operated at full capacity to literally keep Arizona from becoming polluted with aging aircraft, not quite unlike beaches full of beer cans; a poor analogy. Strangely enough the process continues until this very day. True, we have up-graded our methods of destruction and become more sophisticated in the eradication process. Nonetheless, you can visit Davis Monthan AFB, Arizona, and see the once proud fleet of B–58 *Hustlers* neatly lined up in a row silently awaiting their turn to be chopped to pieces and crammed into the careless furnaces.

Just as fast as we put behind us the last generation of aircraft (whether they fought in war or were deterrents in peace, is of no consequence) we also tend to abandon those who flew them, or crewed aboard them, or supported them on the ground, and those who designed and built them. Therein lies the real tragedy.

But fortunately for us the world is a big place and the bureaucratic process has its shortcomings in *some* instances. As a result many of these history making planes managed to get lost in the shuffle. Unbelievably, some were even offered for sale as war surplus material. Between the "mavericks" and those sold, a fair assemblage of aviation's history from 1939 through 1945 (and later, too) has been salvaged for personal use of one type or another, and/ or posterity. While it is rare, it is not altogether uncommon to round the corner in some relatively unknown city or town and suddenly come face-to-face with a deadly looking World War II fighter usually cocked at an angle atop a stone or iron pedestal. Others lie unnoticed in falling down barns or in unkept sections of fields . . . awaiting to be found. In recent years a sense of urgency has pervaded certain segments of our flying community that is sensitive to the need of preserving aircraft that flew in that era of our aviation history.

Because of their fierce dedication it is now possible for people from the world over to see and marvel at historical items that would have certainly perished forever had it not been for this handful of men. Museums now exist all over the world. None are complete, but each presents at least one aircraft not found in any of the other museums. The analogy would be to libraries . . . some are limited, but good, while others are amazingly well rounded out in their inventory. Some deal strictly with Naval aircraft, some are faithful to USAF types while others concern themselves with either foreign built planes or a hodgepodge of them all.

But one thing is certain. With the passing of each day attrition rears its ugly head to take not only one or more of the precious treasures of flying history but also those souls who put them in the air and those numberless ones who rolled them off production line.

Eventually all of the people will be gone . . . not so with the aircraft to which they related. Archivists, museum curators and hard-headed individuals will see to it that most of these planes will survive through the ages.

Thousands of excellent books have been written about these great aircraft. From them, an in-depth knowledge is gained. Some of these writings will survive for generations to come. Countless photographs taken during these years exist. Most, however, were static or were candid in nature, and many were poor in quality or point of view. During the fast pace of action it was a very unwise person who attempted to capture the event on film. And if he did the result was invariably poor.

The artist closes the gap and focuses attention on the high-point or interesting feature of an aircraft type or a particular action. Working with pilot's de-briefing reports, good to bad unit histories, and most important . . . effecting face-to-face confrontations with one or more persons directly involved, a true historical event can be visually recorded and supported with the complete story. Done properly, such an endeavor can be perpetuated indefinitely.

This book has been designed to last for generations. The pendulum swings from doves to hawks. As a short-range consideration this book can easily fall within either camp, despised by the one, eagerly sought by the other. In the long pull it will be accepted for the original intention, which has been to add to the historical accounting of that great conflict. In the end this Epilogue should fall within the same frame of reference as all other accounts of our heritage and, in part, some of that of both our allies and our enemies.

ABOUT THE AUTHOR

Glenn Bavousett lives with his wife, Jennie, and the youngest of three sons, Leslie, in the rural horse-raising and farming community of Keller, Texas. Glenn doesn't remember when he became hopelessly attached to airplanes. His great dream was to fly with the Navy but that urge quickly disappeared one morning at boot camp in San Diego when he saw two planes collide. He went on to become a radarman and participated in several amphibious assault actions in the Pacific. After the war, Glenn remained in the service, transferring to minesweeper duty and then to the U.S.S. *Blue Ridge,* one of three close-range observation ships for the experimental atomic bomb blasts ("Operation Crossroads") at Bikini atoll.

All of his adult working career has been in the aerospace industry, especially in technical data preparation. Glenn has worked as technical illustrator at General Dynamics, Bell Helicopter Company and LTV Aerospace. He is an ex-chairman of the Fort Worth, Texas, Chapter of the Society of Technical Writers and Publishers.

While art and writing are his "druthers," Glenn is a competitive pistol shooter, racing sailboat crew member and a Colonel in the Confederate Air Force.

ABOUT THE ARTIST

Tony Weddel is a product of the aviation oriented Dallas-Fort Worth community. He was born in Fort Worth during World War II, on March 9, 1942.

As a photographer's mate stationed at the Naval Air Station in Dallas, Texas, during the early sixties, Tony began to get the "feel" of the excitement and tensions of aerial warfare from an almost endless supply of gun-camera films and other World War II combat footage shot for historical purposes. His environment at NAS Dallas naturally brought him in close contact with airmen who fought during the "big" war or were knowledgeable of events of that conflict.

Tony has not always been a combat aircraft illustrator. Bypassing both the usual college art courses and pure art schools, he first tackled heavy construction work, a far cry from the tender stroke of a sable-hair brush; then slowly he entered into a career in art. After receiving initial exposure into the "real life" of practical illustration in a couple of art studios, he moved into the religious art field where he designed magazine covers and did artwork for inside story spreads and cover designs for record albums.

With the local aerospace industry badly needing illustrators, Tony shifted into the highly specialized disciplines of a technical illustrator, where he learned to read engineering data and convert that information into pictorial form for easy comprehension by layman. Coupling his technical skills with a talent for generating conceptual art, it was an easy and natural step for Tony to begin creating meaningful combat aircraft scenes.

In 1969 Tony was recognized by his contemporaries within the local area by being named "best artist" of the year, a result of two acrylic paintings depicting A7 *Corsairs* and F4H *Phantoms*.

141

Weddel's aircraft illustrations have been treasured possessions of Mrs. Anna Chennault; General Nathan Twining; Princess Catherine Caradja of Rumania, who saved an appreciable number of Allied airmen downed over Ploesti; General Catton, Chief of the Military Air Command; ex-Sergeant Eddie Holland, now of the Division of Aeronautics, State of Arkansas; Bob Hoover of North American Aviation; and Colonel J. A. Gunn.

Tony immerses himself in his work; his love of fishing from some quiet bank is more often than not replaced by the magnetism of model aircraft building, the sketching of aircraft or his other love—western art.

INDEX